101 Improv Games
for Children and Adults

"Bob Bedore and his troupe, Quick Wits, are synonymous with improv in Utah. His passion for legitimizing improv as entertainment in Utah has been felt for the past nine years. Bob is unafraid of taking chances onstage, whether it is with people or with a new take on a game or an idea. Audiences and fellow actors alike have constantly been thrilled and entertained by his antics and risk-taking. This is a man who emphasizes that everyone is brilliant onstage, and then goes up there and proves it."

— Jesse Parent
Editor of UtahImprov.com

"This book is a useful tool for teaching improv. I have been integrating improvisation into my teaching for five years and am always impressed by the way it taps into children's natural curiosity and openness to the infinite possibilities of the world around them. Improvisation allows children to use their imagination to explore and engage their environment and relationships in a way that no other performance art does. It shows them the power of agreement, possibility, and the creative human spirit."

— Will Luera
Artistic Director of ImprovBoston

Smart Fun Books from Hunter House

101 Music Games for Children by Jerry Storms

101 More Music Games for Children by Jerry Storms

101 Dance Games for Children by Paul Rooyackers

101 More Dance Games for Children by Paul Rooyackers

101 Drama Games for Children by Paul Rooyackers

101 More Drama Games for Children by Paul Rooyackers

101 Movement Games for Children by Huberta Wiertsema

101 Language Games for Children by Paul Rooyackers

101 Improv Games for Children by Bob Bedore

101 Life Skills Games for Children by Bernie Badegruber

101 More Life Skills Games for Children by Bernie Badegruber

101 Cool Pool Games for Children by Kim Rodomista

101 Family Vacation Games by Shando Varda

101 Relaxation Games for Children by Allison Bartl

101 Quick-Thinking Games + Riddles for Children by Allison Bartl

101 Pep-Up Games for Children by Allison Bartl

404 Deskside Activities for Energetic Kids by Barbara Davis, MA, MFA

Yoga Games for Children by Danielle Bersma and Marjoke Visscher

The Yoga Adventure for Children by Helen Purperhart

Yoga Exercises for Teens by Helen Purperhart

The Yoga Zoo Adventure by Helen Purperhart

Ordering

Trade bookstores in the U.S. and Canada please contact:

Publishers Group West
1700 Fourth St., Berkeley CA 94710
Phone: (800) 788-3123   Fax: (800) 351-5073

Hunter House books are available at bulk discounts for textbook course adoptions;
to qualifying community, health care, and government organizations;
and for special promotions and fund-raising. For details please contact:

Special Sales Department
Hunter House Inc., PO Box 2914, Alameda CA 94501-0914
Phone: (510) 865-5282   Fax: (510) 865-4295
E-mail: ordering@hunterhouse.com

Individuals can order our books from most bookstores,
by calling **(800) 266-5592**, or from our
website at **www.hunterhouse.com**

1͜01

Improv Games

FOR

Children and Adults

Fun and Creativity with
Improvisation and Acting

WITHDRAWN

Bob Bedore

with photographs by Ian Barkley

A Hunter House $SmartƱun$ **book**

Hunter House Inc., Publishers
PO Box 2914
Alameda CA 94501-0914

Library of Congress Cataloging-in-Publication Data

Bedore, Bob.
101 improv games for children and adults / Bob Bedore.
    p. cm. — (A Hunter House smartfun book)
ISBN-13: 978-0-89793-425-1 (spiral), ISBN-13: 978-0-89793-424-4 (pbk.)
ISBN-10: 0-89793-425-3 (spiral), ISBN-10: 0-89793-424-5 (pbk.)
1. Improvisation (Acting) 2. Games. I. Title: One hundred one improv games
    for children and adults. II. Title: One hundred and one improv games for
    children and adults. III. Title. IV. Series.
PN2071.I5B44 2003
792'.028—dc21   2003012860

Project Credits

Cover Design: Jil Weil
Book Production: Jinni Fontana Graphic Design
Developmental and Copy Editor: Ashley Chase
Proofreader: Lee Rappold
Acquisitions Editor: Jeanne Brondino
Editor: Alexandra Mummery
Publicist: Lisa E. Lee
Foreign Rights Assistant: Elisabeth Wohofsky
Customer Service Manager: Christina Sverdrup
Order Fulfillment: Washul Lakdhon
Administrator: Theresa Nelson
Computer Support: Peter Eichelberger
Publisher: Kiran S. Rana

Printed and Bound by Bang Printing, Brainerd, Minnesota

Manufactured in the United States of America

9 8 7 6 5 4   First Edition   09 10 11 12 13

Contents

Preface   xiii

Introduction: The Basics

What Is Improv?.   1

Where Did Improv Come From?   2

Why Improv?.   5

Teaching Improv to Children   8

Building Blocks for Beginners   12

Key to the Icons Used in the Games   19

The Games

Warm-up Games.   22

Exercise Games   32

Emotional Games   41

Body Games   48

Basic Scenes.   60

Character Games   71

Teamwork   78

Singing Games   86

On Your Toes.   94

Guessing Games.   105

Narrative Games   115

Mind Games   127

Bizarre Games.   132

Line-up Games   141

Bonus Game   149

Antics for the Advanced

Character 152

Environment 158

The Scene 161

Creating Magic 165

Bending the Rules 167

Having Fun 168

Putting On a Show

Forming a Troupe 169

Practice 170

The Emcee 172

The Show 174

List of Games

	Beginner	Intermediate	Advanced

Page   Game

Warm-up Games

Page	Game	Beginner	Intermediate	Advanced
23	Take a Walk	●		
24	What Are You Doing?	●		
26	What Is It?	●		
27	Where Is It?	●		
28	Blind Sculpture	●		
29	Counting on You	●		
30	Fortunately/Unfortunately	●		
31	One-Word Story	●		

Exercise Games

Page	Game	Beginner	Intermediate	Advanced
33	Any Scene	●		
34	Bus Stop	●		
35	Follow the Leader	●		
36	Hitchhiker	●		
37	One-Word Sentence	●		
38	Talk or Die	●		
39	Tag Out		●	
40	Yesman Advertising	●		

Emotional Games

Page	Game	Beginner	Intermediate	Advanced
42	Emotional Scenes	●		
43	Emotional Boundaries		●	
44	Emotional Relay		●	
45	Emotional Storytelling	●		
46	Making Faces		●	
47	Scripted Scene		●	

		Beginner	Intermediate	Advanced

Page   *Game*

Body Games

		Beginner	Intermediate	Advanced
49	Freeze Tag	●		
51	Freeze Tag Forward-Reverse			●
53	Action Figures	●		
54	Bionic Parts		●	
55	Discworld			●
56	Improv Olympics		●	
57	Stand Up, Sit Down, Bend Over		●	
58	Stunt Double			●
59	Helping Hands			●

Basic Scenes

		Beginner	Intermediate	Advanced
61	Animal Soap Opera		●	
62	Between the Lines		●	
64	First Line, Last Line		●	
65	Oscar-Winning Moment		●	
66	Pieces of Paper		●	
67	Fairy Tale News			●
68	Fairy Tale Courtroom		●	
69	Talking Columns		●	
70	Ask the Prompter		●	

Character Games

		Beginner	Intermediate	Advanced
72	Animal Police			●
73	Bad Advice		●	
74	Characters and Objectives		●	
75	Old Job/New Job		●	
76	Here He Comes Now		●	
77	Nightmare Auditions		●	

Page	Game	Beginner	Intermediate	Advanced
Teamwork				
79	Double Date		●	
80	The Oracle		●	
81	Soap Interpreter			●
82	Speak As One		●	
83	Spelling Bee		●	
85	Triple Dub			●
Singing Games				
87	Blues Song		●	
89	Da Doo Run Run		●	
90	Gibberish Opera			●
91	Musical Between the Lines			●
92	Object of Desire			●
93	Three-Headed Monster			●
On Your Toes				
95	Silly Accents			●
96	Film and TV Styles		●	
97	Occupations		●	
98	Shopping Mall		●	
99	Four Ways to Die			●
100	Lie Detector		●	
101	Fiendish Torture			●
102	Superheroes		●	
103	Barnyard Symphony		●	
104	Genre Bending		●	

	Beginner	Intermediate	Advanced

Page	Game	Beginner	Intermediate	Advanced
	Guessing Games			
106	Idiot Poker		•	
107	Late for Work		•	
108	Murder Mystery		•	
109	News Quirks		•	
110	Party Quirks		•	
111	Plea for Help			•
112	The Return Department		•	
114	What Am I Doing Here?		•	
	Narrative Games			
116	Fairy Taled			•
117	Behind the Fairy Tale			•
119	"A&E Biography"			•
121	Coming Attractions			•
122	Playing Creator		•	
123	Paperback Writer			•
125	Slideshow		•	
126	History Bluffs			•
	Mind Games			
128	Dr. Seuss		•	
129	Questions? Anyone?			•
130	Short Attention-Span Theater (SAS)		•	
131	Shake Up Your Shakespeare			•

Page	Game	Beginner	Intermediate	Advanced

Bizarre Games

133	Ball of Mucus			●
134	Bucket of Water			●
136	Dead People			●
138	Evil Twin			●
139	Hecklers		●	
140	Superhero Eulogy			●

Line-up Games

142	Bunch of Blanks			●
143	Wearing Many Hats		●	
144	Hot Spot		●	
145	Pile of Props		●	
146	Scenes Not Seen		●	
147	Unlikely Slogans		●	
148	World's Worst		●	

Bonus Game

149	Storython			

Preface

I remember my first introduction to improv clearly. I'd like to say it feels like yesterday, but it was nowhere near yesterday.

I was a sophomore in high school, sitting in a beginning drama class. I had no idea I would like acting—I only took the class because my dad told me to. We had just moved, and I was depressed about leaving behind all of my friends. My dad said that lots of outgoing kids would be in the drama class. In short, he was trying to find a way to help his son make some new friends.

So there I was. The teacher said that we were going to do something called improv. There was no real introduction. The teacher just picked a few students, myself among them, and said, "You're all dogs in a dog pound." Soon all of the students were impersonating dogs, barking, howling, and panting.

Something struck me. I leaned to one of the other dogs and said, "I'm breaking out of here tonight. Are you with me?" The other dogs looked at this "talking dog" for a moment, and then realized that they could be just like me. Soon we had all put together a tight, and funny, plan to escape. The energy of that moment has stuck with me to this day.

Soon I changed from a guy who only wanted to be a sports writer to one who lives for the stage. Oh, I've tried to pull away. I even went to the University of Utah on a journalism scholarship and became the assistant sports information director. But if you're reading this book, you know theater is something you can never break away from. In 1994 I started an improv comedy troupe now known as Quick Wits. We specialize in quick, fun, in-your-face improv. I've performed improv almost every weekend for nine years, and I never get tired of it. And now I'm able to express my love for improv in this book. If only a part of my enthusiasm and passion for this art form rub off on you— as opposed to the ink—I'll be happy. And you'll have a lot of fun.

So what should you expect to find between the covers of this book?

Part One examines the basics of improv. The first few sections explain what improv is, where it came from, and why it's important. Next comes a special section on teaching improv to children. The final, and most important, section in Part One outlines some rules and tips for improv beginners. These rules are the building blocks improvisers can use to create a scene from nothing. Even if you are a seasoned improviser, I recommend you at least glance over these rules. After ten years of performing I find that I can always learn something new.

Part Two contains the games. Our Quick Wits playbook currently has over 400 games that we have played on our stage, so picking 101 of them was a real chore. I've chosen a mixed bag of games for beginning, intermediate, and advanced players. There are even a few near-impossible games to give you a full overview.

Part Three describes some of the advanced techniques we use in Quick Wits to give each scene an added punch. We'll also examine how to bend many of the rules I laid out in the Beginners' section. It's all designed to help experienced improvisers "think outside the Black Box."

Finally, in Part Four, we look at some of the elements that go into creating a successful improv show. You'll learn how to assemble a troupe, conduct rehearsals, and put together a show. I'll also discuss the essential role of the emcee.

I hope you'll enjoy the journey. My journey has taken me from the boy in high school to a veteran with more than twenty-three straight years of performing onstage. In all those years I have never gone more than three months without being involved in some type of show. While onstage I have had the great fortune to meet my beautiful wife, make some of the most loyal friends anyone could ask for, and even act with my three children. I've acted in movies, hosted a children's television show for two years, worked in radio for twelve years, owned theaters, and had more fun than should be allowed.

Not bad for a guy who is still doing nothing more than planning his escape from the dog pound.

Bob Bedore
February 2003

For easy reading we have alternated use of the male and female pronouns. Of course, every "he" also includes "she," and vice versa.

Introduction
The Basics

What Is Improv?

Improv is producing something onstage from little more than a suggestion and your own imagination. Improvisers build a scene from nothing. Characters interact, solve problems, love, hate, and basically live their lives in a heartbeat. Improv characters are like flies—they spend their short life span beating their wings as fast as they can and living as if they'll go forever, not really knowing that their time is short.

For actors, improv is the ultimate teaching tool. Acting is all about reacting—responding naturally to what has been said or done onstage. Since acting is reacting, there is nothing that will build your acting skills faster than improv. In a scripted scene your character's reactions have already been mapped out. In an improv scene it's all up to you. The actor has complete control over every action and thought of her character—there's no director and no writer. Do you want to have your character suddenly open a portal to another dimension and climb through? You can. An improv scene can be played again and again with the same setup, but one word can change the scene in ways no one could have imagined. It's a rush that is hard to explain until you've done it.

Improv is like jumping out of an airplane and just grabbing whatever parachute happens to be lying around. You don't know if you've grabbed a good one or not. You don't even know if you've actually grabbed a chute—it could be someone's backpack. The point is: You've jumped, and now you're going along for the ride.

Improv is also the ultimate team-building exercise. I use it in my motivational speaking to show what people can create by listening and reacting. If an improv scene flops, everyone onstage flops equally. Knowing that everyone must go down with the ship is a powerful motivation for people to work together. There are no great "solo" improv actors—they're stand-up comedians. Seeing everyone come together and begin to think as if with one mind is one of the most exciting parts of improv.

Where Did Improv Come From?

Now there's a tough question. I would have to say that cavemen started the form. With nothing more than a few grunts and gestures they were able to tell the story of a great hunt. And knowing human nature, I'm sure that those stories were exaggerated a bit.

They acted out the characters of the hunter and the hunted. They expressed emotion. There was action. There was a beginning, a middle, and an end. It was a scene, and it was performed in front of an audience of enthralled onlookers.

I would give just about anything to be able to watch one of those performances. There must have been some master storytellers in prehistoric times. But, alas, no one will ever know of the great ones. All we have left of them are a few cave drawings and some skulls in the ground. Our loss.

Commedia dell'Arte

Many believe that modern improv descends from commedia dell'arte. This art form was first seen in Tuscany around 1550. Although its exact origins are hard to trace, commedia dell'arte was rooted in the masked comedies of ancient Rome. Commedia dell'arte used a combination of improvised dialog, a few stock speeches, mime, acrobatics, and broad humor to reach its audiences. It influenced the performing arts all over Europe, remaining popular from the Renaissance through the eighteenth century. Even William Shakespeare used commedia dell'arte characters in his comedies. Later, commedia dell'arte started to evolve into other forms, such as vaudeville. This theater style, with its slapstick humor and variety show format, became popular in North America during the nineteenth and early twentieth centuries. Vaudeville theater is a direct descendant of commedia dell'arte. For example, the popular vaudeville "doctor" skits owe everything to the commedia dell'arte character Dottore, the doctor. Our modern day clowns also come from the same family tree.

Perhaps the most important character in commedia dell'arte is Zanni, the servant. This was the one character who spoke directly to the audience. The performer who played Zanni was often the most talented of the troupe, for he had to be a skillful acrobat and musician as well as an actor and comedian. To this day the word *zany* (derived from Zanni) describes wild comedy.

An entire book could be written about commedia dell'arte—and in fact many have been. I would suggest looking into them for more on this fascinating form. You can also pick up a copy of *Servant of Two Masters* by Carlo Goldoni, a fun commedia dell'arte play.

Modern Improv

Improvisation has been part of theater in one form or another throughout history, but the improv form we enjoy today grew directly from children's games. In Chicago during the Great Depression of the 1930s, an actor and drama teacher named Viola Spolin developed a system of theater games for children. These games were designed to use child's play to stimulate imagination and self-expression. Spolin did not originally intend these games to be performed for an audience; they were meant to be classroom exercises. Spolin's theater games are the forerunners of modern improv, and many of the games she invented are still played today.

It wasn't until Spolin's son, Paul Sills, started tinkering with the games in the 1950s that improv started to come to the stage. He worked with his mother and others to create a staged show that grew in popularity in the Chicago area. The show, called The Compass, continued to expand and in 1959 became one of improv's best-known organizations, Second City.

One of the men who helped Second City become the major force it remains today was Del Close. Close joined in 1960 and later became the driving force for the troupe. He devoted much of his life to the craft and championed "long-form" improv. A long-form improv is a collection of scenes that look at the same suggestion from different angles. It is a free-form style, with no time limit. Close's legacy will forever be tied to "The Harold," a complex style of long-form that even he admits has a strange name.

While Chicago was enjoying its improv renaissance in the 1960s, a native of England was making his own noise in Canada. A professor at the University of Calgary, Keith Johnstone noticed that theater was not reaching the masses. He wanted to create a show that appealed to the same people who enjoyed other activities, like sporting events. Not unlike Shakespeare in his day, Johnstone wanted to reach the common man with art. His creation, Theatresports, combines improv games with a scoring system, adding the mix of competition to the silliness onstage.

There isn't a troupe performing today that doesn't owe at least a nod of thanks to these pioneers.

My Own History in Improv

I first came to improv as a stand-up comedian. A promoter had us do improv from time to time to fill empty spots (when other acts fell through and we needed to fill time). We never tried to be a troupe, but it was by doing this that I learned how to do some improv in front of a crowd. My own improv troupe, Quick Wits, began in 1994. I was opening the Off Broadway Theatre in Salt Lake City and wanted to do something different. There was no improv in Salt Lake City at the time, and all of the actors were pretty nervous about trying this. Oddly enough, the name Quick Wits was originally meant to be a temporary name. I never came up with a name I liked more, and after nine years the name Quick Wits basically stands for improv in Salt Lake. I'm glad I never changed it.

We went through different formats until finally settling on the "competitive" format in 1996. Salt Lake had just been awarded the 2002 Winter Olympics, and I came up with "OlympWits" as a means to capitalize on this. The format took off, and we've done it that way since. Two teams of three actors compete to see who can make the audience laugh most. The people in the audience are the judges, and they score the games. Even so, the teams' real goal is not to win, but to give the audience a good time. We want the people paying to see us to be the real winners. (I know, it's sappy.)

I've performed in a Quick Wits show almost every weekend for the past nine years and have gotten excited for each and every one. The other day I threw my back out and couldn't stand. I was actually in a great deal of pain, and my only thought was that I wasn't going to get to play that night.

Our style is fast and in-your-face. When you come to Quick Wits, you know that laughs are going to come one right after another. Even if a skit doesn't go well, the bits that the actors do between the skits will make you laugh. These actors will do whatever it takes to make the audience laugh. We listen to the audience and notice what gets a positive reaction, so, without knowing it, the audience decides what we do. It's a true "have it your way" experience—fast-food comedy.

Quick Wits was the only improv in town for a while. Then people started seeing how much fun it was and how easy it looked. Troupes started springing up all over the place. Eventually, on any given weekend night you could catch five or six different troupes in a thirty-mile radius—not bad for a city that doesn't usually make a blip on the cultural radar. In a way, I've created my own competition, but I don't worry. In fact, I love to see the other troupes and hope that someday little old Salt Lake will be as well known for improv as Chicago or Los Angeles.

And the Future?

That's where you come in. By showing an interest in improv, and working to pass it on, you are keeping it alive.

Why Improv?

Well, that's the question, isn't it? Why improv? Why indeed.

I've taught improv at almost every level, from preschool all the way to adults. The kids are great. They have a built-in love for imagination and exploration. Sometimes it's the adults who have forgotten where they come from. When I visit university classes, I'm often hit with the same questions: "What is the point of playing games and generally acting like a fool onstage?" "Where is the scene work?" "Where is the character development?" "Where is the serious actor?"

I hate that kind of question. It always makes me feel like some sort of court jester. Improvisers are fine for a laugh, but make way for the serious actors. Blah! As an actor who has done, and continues to do, Shakespeare and loves to do serious dramatic work, I want to pass this one point on.

Not only is improv just as real as "serious acting," but more can be learned about the acting craft in improv than in just about any other technique I've studied. And more importantly, more can be learned about yourself.

Improv has all kinds of benefits, and not only for actors.

Improv teaches you to adapt. I remember another defining moment in high school. We were performing "The Man Who Came to Dinner," and the lights went out right in the middle of the lead actor's speech. The actor didn't skip a beat. He talked as if nothing had happened for about twenty seconds until the lights came back on, and then continued from there. During intermission he was bragging about how he was a true professional because he wasn't shaken by the lights. I asked him if that's what he does at home when the lights go out. Do he and his family just go on about their normal business if the power suddenly cuts out? He didn't see my point, but I made a mental note never to let unforeseen problems take the audience out of the moment. Even if actors are using a script, we have to be ready for the unexpected and willing to adapt. Improv teaches actors to adapt.

But there is more that improv can do for you.

Improv develops confidence, both on the stage and off of it. Knowing that you can adapt will give you confidence in auditions and onstage. Whenever I'm at an audition and the director says, "Now try it like this...," I smile. I already know I've got an advantage over the poor actors who have repeated the same line in the same tone all night to get ready for the audition.

Even those not interested in acting will benefit from improv. Lots of people who take my classes really don't plan to perform onstage. I've taught improv to salesmen who want to learn how to think on their feet. I've taught managers who want to learn how to deal with employees. I've taught several people who only wanted to improve their public speaking.

But children are my favorite improv students. Teaching them is a real joy. Very few of them decide to pursue an acting career, but I can see that each of them has grown from the experience of doing improv. They are not as shy as they were when they started. They seem better adjusted and better able to handle life's twists and turns.

I've had several students who were in that "fat kid" stage. (I was like that and it was tough.) Children like them don't get a lot of praise from the other kids. But then they do something cool in an improv scene, and somehow it doesn't matter anymore. Sometimes I'll even see a kid become confident enough to use his size to his advantage in a scene. And only a few days before he was trying to hide his weight behind the desk. I have also seen shy children break out of their shells and not only interact, but laugh and enjoy themselves. Improv can work miracles like that.

Improv gives people the confidence to step out of their normal daily routine and see where other choices might lead. Children who have taken my classes have taken more risks later in life. I don't mean the self-destructive kind of risky behavior, I mean healthy risk-taking. They might not have thought that they could audition for a lead role before, but now they do. They might not have thought that they could ask someone to dance before, but now they have the confidence of Gene Kelly. They have a "why not" attitude. I have taught them the most important rule of improv: You can't fail. The only way you can fail is by not trying.

Improv develops creativity. As children we have a natural ability to use our imaginations, but as we grow older our imaginations often become rusty with disuse. Improv forces you to use your imagination. Nothing happens until you make it happen. And this isn't just practical in the "fun" world of theater. Knowing how to generate ideas, and how to work with others to flesh out their ideas, are very useful "real-world" skills. Students of mine have often pointed to their improv skills as the reason they did well in meetings, sold a house, or got a promotion. Being able to see many sides to a situation as quickly as possible will help you solve all kinds of problems and challenges. Improv helps you look at the world differently.

Improv strengthens speaking and listening skills. It teaches you how to formulate your thoughts quickly and present them well. Improv gives performers ample opportunity to work on diction, expression, and fluency. Listening is essential in improv, as scenes may abruptly change direction. If you are not listening in an improv scene, you will quickly be left behind.

Improv teaches cooperation. As I said earlier, there are no solo stars in improv. Everyone has to work together to create a scene, or it will fall apart. Doing improv together builds a group's mutual trust, and helps them appreciate the different talents of individuals.

Improv promotes tolerance. Doing improv together helps different types of people learn to accept each other. When you're onstage trying to keep a scene going, differences in background, politics, appearance, physical ability, and so on are not important. I always strive to teach that what is on our outsides doesn't matter in improv. I've noticed that when my students are offstage they tend to keep that feeling alive, and I love it.

Once, a girl who was deaf signed up for my improv class. At first I wondered how she would do, since listening is so crucial to improv. I decided that if she had signed up, she must have known what she would be getting into. She used an interpreter to help her "hear" what the other were saying, and she could say her own lines aloud. The kids were a little apprehensive about being in scenes with her at first, but soon they didn't give it a second thought. This girl didn't let deafness slow her down and neither did the other students. Man, I love improv!

Improv makes you a better person. This is pretty bold statement, but one I will stick by. Since our daily lives are unscripted, we are really doing improv all the time. Our reactions to situations create our emotions and prompt our dialog. Improv will give you experience with lots of different imaginary situations and help you control your reactions in real life. Your social skills will greatly improve, and you'll soon see that your life is more fun and less stressful.

The last statement is impossible to prove scientifically, but I have seen it happen time and time again. From my wife and three children, to the members of my troupe, to people in other troupes, to people who come to the classes—I have seen improv make a positive impact on dozens of people's lives.

Improv is about building, not about tearing down. And maybe that simple idea is something that I wish I could spread to everyone.

Teaching Improv to Children

Doing improv with children is one of my greatest joys. They still have all of their imagination intact and are willing to use it right away. In fact, sometimes the hardest part is keeping them on track. If you are teaching children, this is the key: Remember what you were like as a kid. Try to see the world from a child's wide-eyed point of view once again.

With many subjects a teacher might decide to introduce the topic gradually, bringing the students along slowly. But children know how to pretend better than we do, so they are natural improvisers. You'll find that children will take to many of the games quicker than adults. Don't try to slow them down. Let them run and give them as much space to experiment as they want. As a teacher your main job will be to focus their energy.

When a class is filled with particularly eager students, I like to introduce a lot of games quickly. In later sessions I go back and work on each game in greater depth. This gives the kids lots of material to work on at home, and I can fine-tune it in class.

Each game takes about five minutes to play, but of course a game will take longer if you play several rounds to give each student a turn.

Too Much and Too Little

When it comes to improv, most children seem to fall into one of two very different categories. First is the child who is a little too eager. Of course, being eager is wonderful. But these kids don't want to find out about how to play a game, they just want to get in there and do it. With these children, every skit seems to turn into a chase or a wrestling match. They just have a bit too much energy. I have found that the best way to keep these kids under control is to act in skits with them myself. That way I can help keep them on track and focused on the scene. Over-eager kids will calm down and focus after they understand how a scene can be played.

The other type of student is the one who isn't sure she wants to be a part of this type of thing. I can understand these children easily. They are afraid to look silly, and improv is a bit overwhelming to some. These students have to be brought along slowly. Never force them into playing a game, because one failure could set them even farther back.

I suggest letting these children start with games that won't put them in the spotlight at all. You might let them try One-Word Story (Game #8) or Fortunately/Unfortunately (Game #7). Afterwards, point out how well they played these games. This will usually get them interested in taking the next step—games that challenge them to portray a character onstage.

Also keep in mind that some children are not comfortable with their bodies. When a class is first starting out, I avoid games that involve touching. It takes a little time to break through this discomfort, so keep on eye on your students and don't put ones who are a bit awkward about touching into uncomfortable situations. This goes for scenes about love as well. When you do decide to introduce games that involve touching, make sure students understand they must treat each other with respect. (And, of course, be sure to follow any guidelines your school may have regarding touching in the classroom.)

Go carefully with cautious children: If they lose their confidence, it will be hard to get it back. Build their confidence, and anything can happen.

It's Okay to Fail

This is the most important point to teach children about improv: It's okay to fail. It doesn't matter what happens onstage. Everything that happens is exactly what should have happened.

You'll see that in order to do an improv scene, each actor has to treat the others onstage as if they are geniuses. If every actor is following this example, nothing done or said onstage can be incorrect. Make sure the entire class understands this point, so that students will work hard to build each other up.

Even if the whole scene falls apart, make sure to find the things that went right and don't dwell too much on the negative. The key is not to make students feel bad about any choices they make onstage. They were the ones who had to make that quick decision, and they will know when it was the wrong one and likely avoid it in the future. If not, just pull them aside quietly and talk to them.

The key in teaching children is: Don't give up on them, and they won't give up on you.

A Week of Improv

If you teach kids regularly in an acting class or similar setting, you can give them a terrific introduction to improv over a week of classes. Here is an outline of how you might structure the week.

Day One. The main obstacle to overcome in improv is the fear of doing it. I help students overcome this fear by showing them how easy it can be. Bring a few kids up and put them in a line. You are going to play One-Word Story (Game #8) with them. Choose an animal (such as a cat) and an occupation (such as garbage collector) and have the kids work together, following the game instructions, to tell a story about a cat who works as a garbage collector. They will put together a very strange story. Ask the group if any of them had that type of plot in mind before the story started. It is likely that none of them did. Point out that what they've just done is an improv—a scene with no preconceived thought, a scene everyone worked together to build.

Now you can begin explaining the beginners' rules to improv, outlined in the next section of this book. Stress teamwork and listening to each other. Let them play the game again and see how it goes. Show them that in improv you're a part of the whole. The scene is about the team and not the individual.

Finish off the first day with a few more games. You might choose What Are You Doing? (Game #2) and Fortunately/Unfortunately (Game #7). The goals are to help students overcome their fear of making up scenes, and to replace that fear with excitement.

Day Two. The second day can be spent experimenting with creating a cohesive scene. Explain to students what makes up a scene—characters; a setting; and a plot with a beginning, a middle, and an end. Now you can have them act out Any Scene (Game #9). Discuss the game afterwards, helping students identify the basic elements of the scene and talking about the rules of improv. This is a good time to move on to the Emotional Games. In fact, Emotional Scenes (Game #17) is one of the best games to use for students learning scene work. Spend the rest of the class working on Emotional Games. See how the students build their excitement by watching each other and trying to make each other laugh.

Day Three. By now students will be over most of their fear of improv and will want to expand. Use the body games to get them used to being physical—moving around onstage and using their bodies. Freeze Tag (Game #23) is a great way to learn this and a lot of fun to play. Now start to put it together with physical guessing games like Late for Work (Game #70) and Murder Mystery (Game #71). These games are often students' favorites and will help them start to bring everything together.

Day Four. By the fourth day you are ready to work on adding environment to a scene. Improv is performed on an empty stage, but Where Is It? (Game #4) will help students realize that they can make the audience believe the bare stage is anything and anywhere. Move on to Pieces of Paper (Game #36) and then let them try some quick-moving games like Lie Detector (Game #64) or Four Ways to Die (Game #63).

Day Five. Now you can try any games you think the students might enjoy. Often they want to go back and play some of the games they've done earlier in the week. Go through the remaining games in the book and let the students run wild.

After a week's introduction, you can go back to improv whenever the mood strikes. The students will be very happy to replay some of their favorites as well as try out some new games.

If you only have one day to try to teach your kids about improv, I have a few suggestions. First, try to find a little more time. The students will want to learn more than you can cram into one class. If more time is not available, do what you can. Just start with the basics from days one and two above, and then let the students know where they can find more information. Encourage them to experiment with improv on their own. Then, when you have a little more free time, give them another shot of improv in class.

Working with Younger Children

If you are trying to teach improv to a particularly young group, and you're not sure whether they'll "get it," you can start with some exercises that are a little easier for them to grasp.

I like to get young children started by telling them about the secret, invisible pocket that all actors have with them. If I reach into this pocket, I can pull out anything I want. First I take out my invisible ball. It has weight to it; I can toss it back and forth in my hands; I can even bounce it off a far wall and catch it. Then I'll toss it to one of the children and, without being told to do so, the child will likely catch it and throw it back. We're interacting. Next I show them that the ball can be made of anything, and it can be as big or as small as I want.

They've just started acting. Now I find out what all the kids keep in *their* invisible pockets. I have them pull out whatever they want. I love the look in their eyes when they "see" what they've brought out. It is amazing. We spend a few minutes on this to help the kids understand that we're just playing—something they do every day. Then we move on to other exercises, such as acting out different animals or emotions. I let them act out what it might be like to walk around in different environments (on a sticky floor or in low gravity, for instance). Now I usually find that they want to do more with improv.

I then slowly start to introduce some of the warm-up games to give them a better sense of what improv is like. Soon they are all having a great time creating wonderful worlds. Just get children started in some fashion, and they'll become a snowball rolling down a hill. I've seen it happen more times then I can count, and I always look forward to the next snowball.

Building Blocks for Beginners

Erasing the Fear

The greatest obstacle for beginners is improv-phobia. People find improv scary. You're creating a scene—without a script—with no real direction. It can't be done!

Well, of course it can be done. It's been done for many years, without a single death that I'm aware of. So how do you get people (or yourself, if you're brave enough to admit it) past the fear and on to the fun? The answer lies in magic.

You see, improv is much like a magic trick. When a magician saws his assistant in half, it looks very real and impossible. It is much the same when improvisers start with nothing and create a full scene. Both magician and improviser owe the awe their acts inspire to the same two secrets: One, the audience thinks it's something they could never do. Two, there's a trick to it.

The audience never realizes that improvising—coming up with words on the spot—is something everyone does every day. There's no script for our daily routine. You didn't study your lines last night in hopes of not fouling up that important bank transaction scene after lunch. In fact, the only time we're not doing improv is when we're acting in a play, and we all know how much we sweat over learning our lines. Compared to that, improv is a snap.

Try this quick exercise. I've just come up to you and asked if you'd like to go and get some tacos right now. What's the answer that just came to your mind? Why did it come so quickly? Maybe you said yes because you were hungry. Maybe you said no because you're a vegetarian. Maybe you said, "How about burgers?" because you're hungry, but don't like tacos. Maybe you said, "I'm covered in packing popcorn" because you didn't hear the question. Whatever you said, you just started an improv scene. It flows from there. And, yes, it really can be that easy.

But how do you take improv from a simple discussion about the merits of fast food and turn it into something people want to watch? What is the trick?

We turn to the magician for the answer. Before a magician can perform in front of a crowd, she has to understand the rules of the trick she is performing. The rules make the difference. Follow them and everyone is amazed. Don't follow them and you've got a very unhappy assistant.

The Rules of Improv

There are those who will ask why you need rules when you are making something up. In fact, I myself believe in bending all of the rules that I'm about to impart to you. But just think about learning to ride a bike. You have to learn how to ride on training wheels before you go to a two-wheeler, and then it's some time before you really feel comfortable riding that bike beyond the view of your house. So it is with improv: First learn to crawl, then to walk. After that you can run to comedic greatness.

The rules are in no particular order, since you have to follow all of them at once to make a scene work. You might find other improv rules somewhere else. If they make sense to you, add them to these and use them. To be truly great at anything, you have to learn from as many sources as possible. This book is just one source, but it's a pretty good starting point.

Stop, Look, and Listen

There is one central concept that underlies all of these rules: teamwork. Teamwork is the most vital part of any improv scene. To work as a team, players must always listen to each other and be aware of what is happening around them. Saying the "perfect line" will do you no good if it turns out that your partners have switched locations on you while you were thinking it up. As an improviser you must be "in the scene" rather than "in your head."

Go back to the taco question. You knew what to answer because you heard my question (all except for that packing-popcorn guy, that is). Keep in mind that you must always be a part of the scene and you've got this rule beat.

Everyone Onstage Is a Genius

This rule is one of my favorites. If everyone onstage is a genius, then there are no wrong answers in improv. And if you think about it, "no mistakes" means that improv can be pretty easy and stress-free. At least that's the way I see it.

It doesn't matter who is onstage with you, you must treat everything they say or do as if it is the most wonderful thing that could be said or done at that moment. In short, it is brilliant! And they, in turn, must treat everything you say or do the same way. This is how you make a team.

Members of my own troupe have argued this rule with me, complaining about someone's lack of improv talent. I always respond: "If you are so much better than X, prove it to me and make X look good in the next scene." Then they go out and have a great scene. I know they are thinking that they just showed me how much better they are than X. To my mind, though, I just saw teamwork onstage. Everyone is happy.

Here's an exercise to help students understand that everyone in the class is important. Take one student and stand him on a chair. Let the class know that this person is the most important person in the class. Make sure the class understands that you are serious. Have them repeat the name of the most important person in the class. Then tell the class that this person cannot ever touch the floor. It is their duty to carry the person to the other side of the class and back. Ask the class if they can do this. Ask them if they're ever going to let him drop. Once the class is set, ask the person if he trusts the class. If he does, he should turn away from them and slowly fall back from the chair, letting the class lift him up and move him around. As the leader you have to keep reminding the class of the seriousness of what they are doing. Also keep reminding them that their thoughts should only be about the person they are holding. Give everyone a chance to see what it feels like to be the ultimate center of attention.

Don't Try to Be Funny...Alone

Keep in mind that improv doesn't have to be funny. There are many wonderful "serious" improv groups out there. Most of them use improv to teach about such topics as social awareness and tolerance. Even though my expertise is in the field of comedy improv, I think that this rule can still apply to any form of improv.

When I teach classes I will write, "Don't try to be funny" on the board. Then I'll add "alone" later to make a point. And that point, once again, has to do with teamwork.

All the players onstage must remember to work together. The scene as a whole is more important than any one joke, and even the funniest jokes won't work if they are out of place in the scene. I have seen so many jokes ruined onstage because one person tried to push it even though the moment had passed. The person even knows the moment has passed, but she is so sure that the bit will be funny, she goes ahead and does it anyway. Then she gets mad because she thinks that the others ruined her joke, but in reality, the others are just going along with the natural progression of the scene.

So if you have a great line, save it. You'll get another chance to use it, believe me. I have a whole file cabinet in my brain filled with wonderful, sidesplitting lines that I have stored up for use at the right time.

The corollary to this rule is "Try to be funny as a team." When players work together, they can set each other up for jokes and funny bits. Nothing is better than knowing the people you are onstage with so well that you can can give your teammate a slow pitch and know that she is going to slam it out of the park as easily as she would a ball on a tee.

Don't Ask Questions

Nothing is worse than watching two improvisers asking a steady stream of questions. Something along the lines of, "What do you want to do?" "I don't know, what do you want to do?"

Or the even more thrilling, "Want some tacos?" "What kind of tacos?" "What kind do you like?" "What kinds are there?" and so on.

Obviously, a few questions have to be asked from time to time in a scene, but the point is to answer them, not add more. Questions are the crutch that many beginning improvisers try to lean on. Kick the crutch away and make players stand on their feet as soon as possible.

No Clipping

In football, clipping, or illegally blocking a player in the back, carries a heavy penalty on the field. It's dangerous because the player can't see the block coming, so it takes him by surprise. In improv, "clipping" means taking another player by surprise, in effect, stabbing her in the back. Clipping is also illegal in improv, and carries a heavy penalty.

The easiest way to explain clipping is to use an example: Two players are onstage. One turns to the other and says, "Hey, we just got a letter from the president. Read it." The second player now has to come up with the contents of the letter off the top of her head.

You won't win many friends in an improv troupe this way. Clipping usually makes the other player look unprepared, and that's never a good idea in improv. It also stops the scene for a bit while thoughts are formulated.

Beginning improvisers often clip when they don't know what to do in a scene. They are trying to put the ball in someone else's hands. Like asking questions, clipping is a crutch.

There are many forms of clipping a player. You can make him dance, sing, do a silly voice, or recite a poem. As a beginner you should always avoid this kind of action. Improv is about being a member of a team and you would never clip someone on your own team.

Instead of forcing someone to do your bidding, do it yourself. If you want to get a letter from the President, open it and read it yourself. You brought it up, it's up to you to finish. If your fellow player wants to add something, he can grab the letter from you and read on.

First Come, First Served

This is another rule that I like to stress. "First come, first served" means that whoever starts a scene sets into motion something that cannot be stopped. It can be altered a little, but not stopped.

If the scene is set on a farm and the first player has started collecting eggs, don't come onstage and say, "I thought this was a dairy farm." After the scene has been established, all other interpretations of that scene are put on hold or put aside completely. There's no need to think about something else you could be doing. You are already in the middle of a scene. Just go with it.

After you've done improv for a while you'll realize that you hear the same scene suggestions being given time and time again. Save your idea of a variation on the current suggestion for the next time it's brought up. I have a second filing cabinet in my brain for scene suggestions, right next to my filing cabinet for one-liners.

Never Say No

This is the rule that many point to as the most important rule in improv. I both agree and disagree. (See Part Three for more on bending the rules.) But I do think it's essential for beginners to understand this rule and follow its spirit at all times.

"Never say no" means that a player should never come right out and deny something that someone has stated. If a teammate asks, "Why do you have a duck on your head?" you can't reply, "I don't have a duck on my head," because if you do, you will take everyone (onstage and in the audience) out of the scene. The action will come to a complete stop. And from that point on no one knows who is telling the truth. If you don't want to have a duck on your head, simply take it off and say, "Sorry, I forgot I put that there," and then move on with the scene.

This rule is often referred to as the "Yes, And" rule. "Yes, And" is a rule of acceptance. For instance, let's say you and your partner have to do a scene about shopping at the mall. You have a great idea about something funny happening at a record store, but your partner starts off by saying, "Let's go to the food court." You really want to go to the record store, but you can't just say, "No, let's go to the record store," because that would completely negate your teammate's idea about the food court.

In comes the "Yes, And" rule like a superhero to save the day. All you have to do is say, "Yes, and afterwards we can go to the record shop." You have slyly communicated with the other player, without letting the audience know it. You've just told the player, "Yes, we shall see what your little food court excursion has in store, but take notice that I have plans for the record shop that could pay big dividends as well." Okay, no one really talks like that, but the point is made.

Putting It All Together

For those paying attention, all the rules of beginning improv break down to one important concept. Remember what that is?

TEAMWORK!

Good for you, you've been paying attention. Or you read the answer without first trying to come up with an answer yourself. Either way, the answer is the same.

As long as all the players are trying to keep the scene moving forward, they will reach the goal. Will it be a great improv scene? That depends on what your definition of a great scene is. For me, every scene following the rules is brilliant!

The best way to introduce these rules is with a demonstration. Don't mention any of the improv rules before you begin. Give players a very general situation to act out in a scene, and watch them carefully. Without making any comments, pay attention to any rules they break in the scene, and think about how the broken rules affect the scene. When the scene is finished, discuss it with the group. Let them talk about how the scene went, and any points in the scene when they felt uncomfortable. They might not know that things were going wrong, but they will feel that something different happened.

Now go over the rules with them, referring to examples of good and bad choices in the scene they just performed. Stress the importance of working together. Have players perform another scene and see if they improve. This time, if they break the rules they should be able to feel it. It will seem as if they've run into a brick wall. Once they start to get a handle on the rules and the reasons why the rules exist, players will start to follow them without thinking. It's like driving—at first it's hard and there are so many rules, but after a while you're able to do it while eating, talking on the phone, or putting on makeup.

Let Them Play

This is a special rule for teachers and directors. The improv rules are important, but don't stop beginners every time they make the slightest mistake. Players have to feel as if there are no mistakes if they are going to explore.

I personally hate to see directors who stop students every single time they ask a question, say "no," or make a choice that the directors themselves wouldn't make. Absolutely no good is achieved by this. You can argue that students need to see where a mistake was made, but I don't buy it. Let the scene play out and see if students can work out of any perceived "mistake." If they do, great! If not, then they'll know it and they won't like the feeling. It is likely that they won't make the same mistake again. And you can always talk about the "mistake" after the scene has reached its ending. Too often I've visited classes where beginners spend all their time looking out of the corner of their eye at a director, checking to see if they're going to be stopped. This makes improv too stressful.

Remember, everyone onstage is a genius, and everything said is brilliant!

Even if it isn't.

Now Perform Magic

It's time to try some of the Warm-up and Exercise Games in this book. This will give everyone a feeling of confidence and a chance to test their legs in improv. Just like a magician, an improviser must believe that their tricks will work. Gaining this confidence is the first, and biggest, hurdle that improvisers must overcome. Once that is accomplished, anything is possible.

Key to the Icons Used in the Games

To help you find games suitable for a particular situation, all the games are coded with symbols or icons that tell you at a glance some things about the game:

- the level of difficulty

- the number of players needed

- suitability for a small space

- the props required

These are explained in more detail below. Two icons included in other SmartFun books (age level and time) have been omitted here. All of the games take about five minutes to play, and they can be played over and over again to give every member of the class a turn. We have not included age levels for these games, because every game in this book can be (and has been) played by children as young as nine. And though adults or teens might play a game better than children, no one could play a game with more enthusiasm. The kids in my classes always clamor to play the hardest games possible.

Level of difficulty These categories reflect the lowest level of experience necessary for players to enjoy the game. However, even advanced players may learn a great deal, and have a great deal of fun, playing some of the "beginner" games.

= Suitable for beginners

 = For intermediate to advanced players

 = For advanced players only

Number of players Most of the games are best played by a small group of from two to four players. Games that require a specific number of players are marked with that number. Games that are suitable for large groups will be marked as such.

 = pairs

 = groups of three

 = groups of four (and so on)

 = groups of four or more (and so on)

 = best played by a group of two to four players

 = suitable for a large group to play together

Suitability for a small space The games are designed for play on a bare stage or in a large open space. Some are adaptable to a smaller space (such as a classroom filled with desks), and they are marked with the following icon.

 = Game is suitable for a small space, such as a classroom filled with desks.

Whether you need props Most of the games require no special props. In some cases, props, audiovisual equipment, or other materials will enhance the game. These games are flagged with the following icon, and the necessary materials are listed under the Props heading.

 = Props needed

The Games

The games in this book are a sampling of the games we play in Quick Wits shows, along with some warm-ups and exercises. I would love to say that we created all of these games, but that is far from the truth. Some we created; some we found; and some we created but then discovered that other troupes had "created" them as well.

The games are broken up into categories so that similar games are grouped together. This gives you a chance to see the themes these games create and start creating your own games.

These improv games are designed to be led by an **emcee**, or master of ceremonies. In a classroom setting, the teacher can act as emcee, and students who are not performing can act as audience. The emcee introduces each game and explains it to the audience. In performance, most improv games begin with a suggestion from the audience, to make it absolutely clear that players will be making up the scenes on the spot. The audience might suggest a setting for a scene, character types for the players to portray, a basic situation to act out, or any number of variables. The emcee chooses an audience suggestion, starts the game, perhaps changes the game as it goes along, and decides when the game should end.

Each game description is divided into two main sections. One section, **For the Emcee/Teacher,** outlines the basic rules of the game and provides tips for the person leading the game, whether emcee or teacher. The other section, **For the Players,** gives players suggestions on ways to improve their performance. Many of the games also include **Teaching Tips,** advice on teaching the games to children and teens.

When Quick Wits started, we had about a dozen or more games on our play list. Now the list contains over 400 games, and it keeps expanding all the time. Coming up with a new game and playing it onstage for the first time is one of the greatest rushes you can get in improv.

Warm-up Games

The following games are designed to put players into the right mind-set to play harder games. They also help players work on the basics of improv. For instance, Take a Walk (Game #1) gets players used to using their bodies onstage; Where Is It? (Game #4) lets them practice creating an environment on a bare stage using mime and other skills; and Fortunately/Unfortunately (Game #7) and One-Word Story (Game #8) teach them to work together to tell a story.

Sometimes students are reluctant to play warm-up games because they want to jump right into the more intense games. But if warm-up games are used correctly, at the beginning of the teaching process, they can become favorites. In fact, two of these warm-up games, Blind Sculpture (Game #5) and What Are You Doing? (Game #2), have actually made their way onstage for real shows.

These games are also a great way to get the whole class involved, since they can be played by a large group, while many improv games are for just a few players.

Photo by Bob Bedore

Take a Walk

For the Emcee/Teacher: Ask players to walk around the room. From time to time call out a particular emotion or character type and have the players change their walk to show the new emotion or character. Encourage players to exaggerate, making their movements and expressions as "big" as possible. Tell them that anyone watching should be able to guess right away what emotion or character was called out. Help players notice how their movements change instinctively when they act out different emotions. Point out that their hands clench when they are angry, or that they take smaller steps when they are afraid. Once players get the hang of it, speed up the game to give them practice changing emotions and characters quickly.

This game is mainly an exercise for the body, but there are a few variations that will give the players some added fun.

Variations:

- Have each player secretly pick out one person to be afraid of and another to be a "protector." Players should walk around, all of them trying to keep their protectors between them and the people they are afraid of. Now the players are learning to create blocking (where and how an actor moves) to go along with their characters.

- Ask all the players to stand in a tight circle with their eyes closed. They should feel the face of the person in front of them until they are familiar with it. Then have players step back and spread out, keeping their eyes closed. Challenge players to reform the circle as exactly as possible with their eyes closed, finding their partners purely by touch.

Tips for Teaching: After students have made their emotions as big as possible, help them to understand levels of subtlety. For example, it is easy to show in your walk that you are seething with anger, but it is more challenging to show repressed anger in a walk. Give the students subtle emotions to express, and see what they do. This will help them add layers to their characters.

2

What Are You Doing?

For the Emcee/Teacher: This is perhaps the most perfect of all warm-up games, for reasons I'll explain in a moment. Invite a pair of players to stand onstage and assign them two letters of the alphabet—*A* and *B*, for example. One player asks the other, "What are you doing?" and the other player answers with an action phrase. The trick is that there must be only *two* words in the phrase, each beginning with one of the assigned letters: in this case, perhaps "<u>A</u>nchoring <u>B</u>ananas." The first player then acts out the phrase, maybe pretending to toss an anchor from a raft made entirely of bananas. Then the players switch roles and play again. You can add to the fun by giving players more letters to work with, creating three- or four-word phrases.

Tell players not to get stuck trying to think up the whole phrase at once. Encourage them to take the words one letter at a time, without worrying too much about whether the phrase makes sense. Remind them that it's up to the other person to act out the phrase, so they can make up whatever they want.

This game is great because it works both sides of the brain so well—intellectual and creative. On the one hand, your intellect must struggle to come up with words to go with the letters. Believe me, it is very easy to freeze when you're thinking up words: Remember to do it one word at a time rather than trying to come up with the whole phrase. On the other hand, acting out the phrases works the creative side of your brain. I love this game and often play it alone in the car, using passing license plates to get my letters.

For the Players: When acting out a phrase, think of all the different meanings a word can have. A good example is the word *dog*. It can mean a pet or a food (hot dog), or it can be used in slang terms to mean a buddy, an ugly person, or even to tease someone (to dog someone). Be creative—just do it quickly. And don't forget that you can talk while acting out the phrase to help get the point across.

Tips for Teaching: This game is a great way for students to experiment with looking at words in different ways. (See the example of possible meanings for the word *dog* in **For the Players** above.) Remind them about multiple meanings so that they will explore. Don't let them settle on the obvious.

3

What Is It?

For the Emcee/Teacher: This fun little game gets players used to handling objects without making them feel like they have to be expert mimes. Divide the class into small groups and have each group sit in a small circle. Hand one player in each circle an invisible lump of clay. Ask the player to mold the clay into an object, silently act out using the object, and pass the object to the next player. The next player takes the object, uses it for a different purpose, and then mashes up the clay to form a different object. The process goes around the circle for a little while.

Encourage players to make increasingly unusual objects after all of the more obvious ideas have been used up. Make sure that they are using the objects in an effective manner.

Variation: Instead of a lump of clay, hand the players an invisible ball to pass around the circle. Ask the first player to decide what the ball is made of and how heavy it is, using facial expression and body language to show this. Then players pass the ball around. Do they all react to it in the same manner? Let players experiment with this game and see what they can do.

Tips for Teaching: This game helps students learn to use mime to create an illusion of shape and mass. Help the student see that sometimes all it takes to get a point across are little things like facial expressions and gestures.

Where Is It?

For the Emcee/Teacher: In What Is It? (Game #3), players "created" single objects. This game challenges them to create an entire environment out of thin air. Ask one player to enter first, using dialog and mime to show where she is and what she is doing there. For example, the player might be a grocer neatening her bins of vegetables before customers arrive. The other players enter one by one and add to the scene, until all of them are doing something different in the environment.

Variation: Once players have the hang of the game, add to the challenge by asking them to play the same scene again, but this time in silence.

For the Players: The first player should pick a character with a strong personality and/or who plays a pivotal role in order to help set up the location. If the player comes in as just a customer in a store, he does not establish what type of store it is, and that will have to fall to one of the other players. There is nothing really wrong with this, but the creation of a strong "lead" character will help the players to have a solid foundation from the beginning.

Tips for Teaching: This game teaches students how to create an environment with small bits of mime. As in What Is It? (Game #3), help them see that sometimes small gestures are all it takes to get a point across. Players also learn to watch each other as they are performing together, because they must do so in order to develop an environment. This game gives them a feel for the important part each character plays in creating the big picture.

groups of 4+

Blind Sculpture

Props: blindfolds for the members of both teams

For the Emcee/Teacher: This game is a competition, but as in all improv games, the point is to have fun. Bring two equal teams of about four players up onstage. Blindfold everybody except one member of each team: They will be the sculptures. Have the two "sculptures" strike a pose, and explain that each team will race to match its sculpture's pose—but team members can use only touch to figure out what the pose is. The blindfolded players take turns trying to match the pose until they all have it. The first blindfolded player feels the sculpture, figures out the pose and matches it, and then calls out to the next player. The next player does not go directly to the sculpture, however, but instead feels the person who went before them to figure out the pose. Each player in turn uses the player who came just before him as a guide. Everyone holds the poses until both teams are finished, because the team that wins the race in terms of speed may lose in terms of accuracy. It is fun to take off the blindfolds and let everyone see how good the other poses are.

For the Players: The game is simple: The laughs come from the audience's reaction to what is happening. The nervous tension they feel because of the race and the touching onstage gets them to laugh. This game might be well suited to open a show or a second act because of the energy it creates.

Tips for Teaching: This game does a great job of helping students feel comfortable using their bodies. It also helps them forget to feel self-conscious about how they look onstage. You may find that some students feel uncomfortable with the touching aspect of the game. If this becomes a problem, don't play the game until they are ready.

Counting on You

For the Emcee/Teacher: The name says it all. Have the players sit in a circle, and explain that they will count together, one at a time. All of the players should feel free to say the next number whenever they feel inspired, but they must listen and watch each other closely. If at any time two or more players speak at the same time, the counting must begin again at "one." Encourage players to see how high they can count.

Variation: You can add to this little game by having players shut their eyes. Now they must rely on acting instinct alone to make sure they don't call out a number at the same time as someone else.

For the Players: The only way the group can succeed is to start to think as one. Don't try to beat the system by choosing one person to say every other number.

Tips for Teaching: This is the perfect game to use when you find students are talking over each other too much. The exercise helps players learn to look for an opening in the dialog and to sense the subtle clues people give when they are about to speak. Notice how some players take to this game quickly and others don't grasp it as well. This is a good moment for you to see who needs to be given a little more training.

Fortunately/ Unfortunately

For the Emcee/Teacher: Have players stand side by side in a line, facing the same direction. Explain that they will take turns telling the good and bad news in a story. Invite a player at one end of the line to start the story by saying a sentence that begins with the word "Fortunately." For example, "Fortunately, my parachute opened." The next player in line has to tell the bad news: "Unfortunately, I wasn't wearing it when it did." The next player tells the good side again: "Fortunately, I wasn't skydiving at the time." Once you get to the end of the line, start over at the beginning. It's good to have an odd number of people in the line so that they switch the "Fortunately" and "Unfortunately" viewpoints each time around. Let the story go down the line at least twice.

For the Players: Know whether you are "Fortunately" or "Unfortunately" and be ready to go. Make sure that you are listening to how the story is progressing as it comes to you. The story may take twists and turns you don't expect. Also, think about adding twists and turns of your own. The "Unfortunately" side can really change the scene—you could even open a gateway into another dimension. As with most improv games, what you do or say must be accepted and added onto by the other players. Don't be afraid to say something wild.

Tips for Teaching: Encourage students to keep the pace quick. The story should flow naturally, without too many long pauses. This will help the class learn to work as a team.

large group

One-Word Story

For the Emcee/Teacher: As in Fortunately/Unfortunately (Game #7), players stand side by side in a line and take turns telling a story about a topic chosen by you or the audience. This time, however, each player will speak only one word per turn. For example, player one says "once." Player two says "upon." Player three says "a." Player four says "time." And so on. Once you get to the end of the line, begin again at the start of the line. Stop the story when it reaches a satisfying ending.

For the Players: Always listen so you'll be ready. Sell your word—make it sound important. Don't be afraid to put in a strange word if it really does fit. Try not to have too much of a story in your mind, because you only have one word to get it going. Don't be surprised if you spend the whole game saying words like "and," "the," and so on.

Tips for Teaching: This game is a great way to teach players that they have to work together to reach a goal because no one person can be in control. Before players begin, give them a topic or title for the story. When the story is done, ask each player what she originally thought would happen in the story. It's almost certain that none of their guesses came close to the actual plot of the story. As with Fortunately/Unfortunately (Game #7), encourage students to keep the pace quick. The story should flow naturally, without too many long pauses. This will help the class learn to work as a team.

Exercise Games

Exercise games involve more player interaction and are thus are a step up from warm-up games. The games challenge players to develop characters and scenes. You can use games like Any Scene (Game #9) to introduce students to the rules of improv, as outlined in Part One. If students need practice with the "Never Say No" rule, Yesman Advertising (Game #16) is perfect.

These games are not just for students—they have all made it to the stage at one time or another. The exercise games are perfect for beginners who are ready for more of a challenge, as well as for seasoned veterans getting back in touch with the basics.

small group

Any Scene

For the Emcee/Teacher: Put two or more players onstage and let them come up with their own scene. Usually, the first player to talk will establish the setting. And that's it.

See how the players work together. They will get used to having to fill the silence with words or actions, and it will become easier and easier for them. I always remind teachers not to stop the players during a scene. If players make a mistake, see if they can work themselves out of it. You'll be amazed by the way the survival instinct will help them reach an end.

This game is used from time to time to start a long-form improv. (See page 3.)

For the Players: There are no rules to this game, so just keep the scene going.

Tips for Teaching: Use this game to impress upon students the idea that every scene has a beginning, a middle, and an end. Have them look for these stages. Examine a scene and ask students to pinpoint where the middle was. Then have them identify the steps that led to the conclusion.

small group

Bus Stop

For the Emcee/Teacher: Players act out a scene set at a bus stop. Each player makes up his own character and motive, the reason why that character has come to the bus stop. The point of the game is to see how the different types of characters react to each other.

The bus stop should become a virtual "Gilligan's Island" of different character types forced to interact with each other. That being said, make sure that their interactions are true to the story that develops. This game is about the characters' relationships with one another. Encourage players to focus on creating a scene that goes somewhere interesting, rather than just showing off wacky characterizations.

Variation: For groups without much experience creating characters, you can give players the characters they are to play, or have them draw different characters from a hat.

For the Players: Don't break your character or change the character's motivation. You should carry whatever character you choose all the way through to the end.

Tips for Teaching: Examine the characters with the students and decide whether each student played true to their character. Keeping a character true to its intent throughout a scene is the real art of acting.

Follow the Leader

For the Emcee/Teacher: Bring three players onstage, give them a situation, and have them perform a scene about it. Choose one player to be the leader and explain that the others must do everything that player says. Neither of the other two players can provide any suggestions for what to do. After a short while, choose a new leader. Encourage players to change leadership smoothly. For example, the new leader might announce the change by suddenly saying something like, "I have an idea!" Continue until each player has had a few turns as the leader controlling the scene.

This game is not just about giving orders and following orders. It's also about seeing what it's like to rely on one person to come up with everything and what it's like to have that responsibility.

For the Players: When this game is performed in front of an audience, the fun comes from the idea that whenever the leadership changes, the former followers have a chance to get revenge on their "ex-leader." The hardest part of this game usually isn't being the leader, it's trying not to lead when you're the follower. As I said, it's a good way to learn the importance of both leading and following.

Tips for Teaching: This is a good game to help create balance when you feel that some students are hogging the stage. Make sure that when players are followers they remember not to offer ideas about the scene. For this game to work as a teaching tool, there can be only one leader at a time. Keep it that way.

Hitchhiker

Props: four chairs

For the Emcee/Teacher: Create a "car" setting by placing four chairs onstage, two in front and two behind. Invite four players to get into the car and give them all the same character type to play (rock musicians, for example). The players should begin acting a scene as that character type, until another player approaches with her thumb in the air, asking to hitch a ride. The driver pulls over to pick up the hitchhiker. Now there is a clockwise rotation of players: The driver leaves the car, and the player behind him moves up to the driver's seat. The other person in the backseat moves over behind the driver, and the front passenger moves to the back, leaving the front passenger seat open for the hitchhiker. When the hitchhiker sits down, she begins acting out a completely new character type. The other three players must instantly match the new character type and play it until the next hitchhiker comes along.

Encourage players to play characters that are in the same category as the hitchhiker's, not the same person. For instance, if the new character type is a pirate captain, they shouldn't all be pirate captains. One can be the first mate, another can be a cabin boy, and perhaps the third could be a pirate about to mutiny.

For the Players: This game is a favorite with audiences, but to make it work, the characters have to be very big. Don't let the car setting limit you: Do whatever you like with the setting. As the hitchhiker, I have even entered the car as a mole in the "Whack-a-Mole" game, making us all take turns rising up and getting hit with a hammer. As with all rules of improv, the rules of this game can be bent, if not broken outright.

Tips for Teaching: Make sure that the hitchhiker doesn't come in and just say, "I'm a...." The idea is for the hitchhiker to play the character so well that he doesn't have to say what it is. The other players should also just become the character type adopted by the hitchhiker without having to say what they think it is out loud.

One-Word Sentence

Props: tape or chalk for marking spaces on the stage

For the Emcee/Teacher: This game is very close to One-Word Story (Game #8), but with a twist. The players will be creating only one sentence, but they will not necessarily add their words in order. Have a group of about five to seven players stand onstage. In front of them, mark blank spaces along a line on the floor, making sure the number of spaces is the same as the number of players. Have one player move to any spot he wants and stand there, repeating one word of his own choosing. Now the rest of the players take turns choosing spaces and adding their own words. As each word is added, the players start repeating their words in order. This continues until all the players have stepped up to a space on the line and we have a full sentence.

This can be a tough game to play—at least, it can be tough to build a good sentence. The players have to not only get a feel for the sentence that's being built, but also watch for other players who might throw in twists. It's usually up to the last player to tie the sentence together.

Variation: To make the game more challenging, add the rule that the second player has to be at least one space away from the first player. It's too easy to build a sentence when the players are all right next to each other.

For the Players: This game gets harder as it goes, so don't wait too long to step up to a space on the line. Try to go with your first instinct and just step up to the line. Although surprising words can be fun, avoid adding a word that is just too strange.

Tips for Teaching: Since this game increases in difficulty, it does an excellent job of teaching players to go with their first instinct. You can also use this game to demonstrate the improv rule "Don't Try to Be Funny Alone." Students may want to look clever by adding a bizarre word that will mess things up. They will get a laugh from the other students, but the sentence will fall apart. Point out that trying to be funny by yourself will only break up what the rest of the team is trying to do.

Talk or Die

For the Emcee/Teacher: Have players stand side by side in a line onstage and give them a subject to discuss, chosen by you or the audience. Tell them they must speak when you point at them. When you pull your finger away they must stop talking, even if they are midword. Then you point to another player, who must pick up exactly where the last player left off. If a player doesn't speak up quickly enough, or stumbles over her words, the audience has the right to yell "die!" Now the player has to "die" onstage, acting out the last noun or phrase that was said as the cause of death. For example, if a player stumbled over the word *computer*, she would have to act out a death caused by a computer—let's say a computer virus. The player then stays dead on the stage for the rest of the skit. If time allows, play until only one player remains "alive."

Variation: To add another element of difficulty, you can make players "die" if they use the word *decide* or any variation of that word. It's been said that actors just "do" things, they don't decide first.

For the Players: The players must watch and listen to each other to make this game work. Be ready at all times. Don't get caught off guard.

Tips for Teaching: This game is all about listening and feeling the flow of what is going on. Don't let students take too long to speak. They need to develop the skill of speaking whatever comes into their minds without spending time analyzing every word.

Tag Out

For the Emcee/Teacher: Ask the audience to suggest a topic for a scene, and bring a group of players onstage to act it out. As the scene goes on, other players sit on the side and watch for lines or actions that give them ideas for new scenes. For example, a player onstage might mention a movie he watched. A player on the side could then "tag" that player (or all the players) out and begin a new scene acting out the movie. That scene continues until the next tag out.

I like it when each scene flows smoothly from the one that came before it. It's also great to have the first scene keep making an appearance from time to time. In cases such as these, the other scenes are used only to flesh out the main scene even more.

For the Players: Be ready for anything that can trigger a tag out. Examples can be a player onstage mentioning something that someone once said to her, or even how she came into possession of something. Players can prompt for a tag out by saying "I wonder what it would be like if..." or some such phrase.

Yesman Advertising

For the Emcee/Teacher: Remember the "Never Say No" rule on page 17? This is the ultimate "Yes, And" game. Bring a group of three or more players onstage to portray employees of the Yesman Advertising Agency, plus one more player to be a client. Have the audience suggest a product the client manufactures. The client comes to the office because she is looking for an agency to advertise her product, and the employees come up with ideas. What happens is pure energy. Every idea is met with cheers. Everything is brilliant. The best way to describe this game is with an example. Client: "I'm selling ping pong balls and I want to sell a lot of them. I'm thinking I want a spokesperson. Who would you recommend?" Player: "Barney!" Other players: "Brilliant!" Then one of the players who didn't suggest Barney has to explain why it was brilliant: "His eyes look like ping pong balls!" "He loves everyone!" As the game continues, the employees put together a complete ad campaign.

For the Players: Don't introduce additional ideas. Once one is said, that's it. Just say it's brilliant and go with it. There's a temptation to shout out another name or location, but avoid doing this. Just look for your chance later.

Come up with fun advertising concepts. Create a jingle, discover a target market that is untapped, offer a free giveaway to go with the product, and so on. This game is all about energy. Keep moving around the stage as if you are trying to find that perfect answer. You should actually be tired after the game. You should also know that everything you've said has been "Brilliant!"

Tips for Teaching: Make sure that energy stays high during this game. Stress that once a suggestion has been made, it is brilliant—there is no need for an alternative. This helps players learn that every answer in improv is the "right" one. As mentioned above, this is an excellent game for teaching the "Never Say No" rule of improv.

Emotional Games

Emotion is one of the most important acting tools we possess. A character's emotions affect her motivation in a scene, her reactions to others, her entire manner. Becoming a master of displaying emotions is essential to growing as an actor.

When you first teach a group these games, make sure they understand that subtlety is not what you want in the beginning. Each of the emotions should be as big as possible. Players aren't just mad or angry, they are seething! They can't just be sad, they have to be sobbing uncontrollably. Later, as players gain more experience at the games, they can begin to add subtlety.

small group

Emotional Scenes

For the Emcee/Teacher: One of the most basic games (and still one of the best), this game is simply the acting out of emotions. Ask the audience to suggest a situation or the setting for a scene based on an emotion and have players act it out. As the scene progresses, call out various emotions for the players to portray. (This style of game is known as a "call game.") The players must instantly change their emotion to the one you called out, and show the reasons why their emotion has suddenly changed. Keep a watchful eye on the scene and look for just the right moments to call out new emotions. Also keep in mind that each new emotion should be very different than the last. Try to go from angry to sad rather than from disappointed to sad. The game is more entertaining when the emotions change drastically.

For the Players: Whatever the emotion, make it as big as possible. If you are sad, you need to be the saddest person in the world. This holds true with any emotion called for by the audience. But also keep in mind that you need to justify why you're changing your emotion. If you don't recognize the emotion that was called out, just fake it for a few seconds and the emcee will give you another. You can even say, "Boy, I'm feeling very (whatever) right now."

This is a popular game because it is almost guaranteed to work if you make the emotions big and justify them. Just have fun with it and let the emotions guide the scene. Don't try to become too involved, because the emcee will change your emotion and you might not be able to finish anything too deep.

Tips for Teaching: Make sure that, as students focus on exaggerating emotions, they don't forget to keep the scene going. Everything should fit in the context of the scene. With younger students, it is best to stay away from "love" emotions; they just make students giggle or feel uncomfortable.

Emotional Boundaries

Props: tape or chalk for marking boundaries on the floor

For the Emcee/Teacher: This game is a close cousin to Emotional Scenes (Game #17), but this time the players have control over their changes in emotion. Use chalk or tape to divide the stage into three parts and assign an emotion to each section. Have two players come up and act out a scene with a setting or situation chosen by the audience. As they move around on the stage, the players must match their emotion to the area in which they are standing.

For the Players: You are in control. You can switch to a different emotion whenever you want to; just move to the area for that emotion. This gives you a chance to plan ahead. Keep in mind that you can also control the other player in the scene. By giving the other player a little push, or by taking her with you, you can change the other player's emotion. Have fun with this.

The audience loves the changes in emotion, so don't stay in one place too long. Give some thought to where you can go and how you can act. One little gimmick is to straddle two areas and act out both emotions at the same time (both happy and disgusted, for instance).

Tips for Teaching: This game is a little tougher than some of the other Emotional Games because now the players have to think a step ahead. Be sure to choose three very different emotions; that way the players will be able to show the transitions easily.

small group

Emotional Relay

For the Emcee/Teacher: Invite the audience to suggest a situation for a scene. Have the players act out the scene, keeping it very simple and brief. Then have them act out the same scene again, but this time give them an emotion to portray. Repeat the scene three or four more times, each time giving the players a new, bigger emotion.

For the Players: Your first scene should be pretty simple, so that it's not too hard to duplicate. But don't be afraid to do something physical like a slap or a hug. These will take on new meanings when done with a new emotion.

This game is not as rigid as game Scripted Scene (Game #22)—players don't have to repeat every line of dialog verbatim. Still, they should repeat the scene as closely as they can.

Tips for Teaching: Make sure students remember to keep their original scene simple. Too much dialog will make the scene impossible to remember.

large group

Emotional Storytelling

For the Emcee/Teacher: This game has much in common with Talk or Die (Game #14): The players stand in a line side by side, and each must be ready to talk when you point to him. However, this game adds the aspect of emotion. Assign a different emotion to each player before the game begins. Give the players a familiar story to tell (such as a fairy tale), then begin pointing. The audience can suggest both the familiar story and the different emotions.

For the Players: While you are waiting for your turn to speak, stay in your emotion: this will make it easier to jump in. Listen to the story and always think of how your emotion works with what is being said. Concentrate! You want to be ready. When the finger points at you, make sure that your emotion is strong. Come in quickly with your emotion and take the story your way. If possible, try to say things that will make the change in emotion seem natural. If you say something like "That made me feel...," it is easy to change to another emotion, and the crowd will love it.

Tips for Teaching: Help students feel comfortable playing this game. As you make the transitions from one emotion to another, try to choose players who seem ready. You might even help them out by looking at the player you plan to point to, making sure the player is paying attention.

small
group

Making Faces

For the Emcee/Teacher: This is a bizarre little game that hurts after a few minutes of playing it. Based on audience suggestions, give each player an emotion with a strong "face" to it. Each player must make that face and keep it through the entire scene, as if she were wearing a mask. The players' actions should also match their facial expressions. It's like Emotional Scenes (Game #17), but each player in this game shows only one emotion.

For the Players: Make the biggest face possible. Then just play out the emotion and keep the same expression on your face. The real humor in this skit comes from making faces and having to keep them. That is also the source of the pain.

Tips for Teaching: Make sure the players keep their "faces" intact the whole time—and the bigger the better. This will help them stay in the right character.

Scripted Scene

Props: simple dramatic scenes of about six lines

For the Emcee/Teacher: Invite a pair of players onstage and give them a scripted scene to act out. The scene should be very short, with only about six lines. After they act it once, have them repeat the same scene several times with variations. You can change the characters' emotions, or you can make other changes to the scene. You might have players act the scene as mother and rebellious teenage son, as passengers on a sinking ship, or as aliens. You might change the setting, the character types, the characters' motivations or relationships, or anything but the words: The lines must never change.

For the Players: Don't screw up the lines.

Tips for Teaching: Use this game to show students how they can change their characters' motivations, actions, and reactions without using words. Students may feel as if only the words in a scene influence their choices, but this game shows how the characters' relationships, and even their surroundings, can also have a profound effect on the scene. Words said at a party would have a very different meaning spoken in a boxing ring.

Body Games

The body games help players learn to use their bodies in a scene. Players focus on justifying their body position and movement—making sure that every pose, every move, makes some sort of sense. The freeze tag games that begin this section are a great introduction to justification of the body. A staple of improv troupes, these games help players think creatively about body positions.

Other games in this section challenge players to take the way they use their bodies even further, by justifying body position and movement in the context of a coherent scene. These games challenge players to focus on physicality and the narrative thread of a scene at the same time. By working on all of these elements together, players will learn to do bigger and better things each time. They will be taking important steps toward putting a scene together.

The body games are also lots of fun, both for the players and for an audience.

Freeze Tag

For the Emcee/Teacher: Take a topic suggestion from the audience and have a pair of players act out a scene based on the suggestion. When you call "Freeze," the players onstage hold still until two new players take their places and match their poses. The new pair now perform an entirely different scene, based on the positions they find themselves in. For example, if the frozen player was standing with his arms crossed in anger, the new player who matches the pose might decide her arms are crossed because she's wearing a straitjacket, and begin a new scene about a magician's escape trick gone wrong.

Variations:

- Instead of calling "Freeze" yourself, have players watch from the sidelines and let them freeze the game. The player who yells "Freeze" should be the first to speak in the new scene.

- Have the players waiting on the sidelines turn their backs to the players onstage, so that they can't see what pose they will have to match until they turn around. It adds a fun element when the audience sees the look on the players' faces. In this variation, the players really have to think quickly. Players can use the time walking to the position to come up with something.

- When players take over after a freeze, have them hold their positions until you give them a title for the scene. The titles should name ordinary events that will lead to fun scenes, such as "Milking a Cow," "On a Date," or "Job Interview." At Quick Wits we call this variation "Freeze Tag from a Hat," because at each freeze the emcee draws from a basket or hat full of titles. Now the players have to be ready for anything; they are forced to act out the scenes from the titles instead of coming up with their own ideas about how to act their way out of their frozen positions. Some players find this version of Freeze Tag much easier, while some prefer the other versions. I guess it's a matter of taste.

For the Players: While performing your scene, make big movements so that the teacher/emcee can find promising poses to freeze you in. If you are just standing there, the emcee has nothing to work with. The bigger your freeze, the harder it is for the next pair to explain the reason for the position in their scene, so have fun!

When you take over after a freeze, strike the pose and see what comes to mind for the scene. If your partner onstage starts the new scene by talking first, go with whatever your partner chooses. Never say something like, "Oh, I thought we were doing _____," because saying that doesn't take the scene anywhere.

Tips for Teaching: Have students strike some poses before playing the game. Ask them to suggest three different explanations for each position: perhaps the same pose could be swinging a baseball bat, carrying Santa's bag over your shoulder, and boxing your own ear. Encourage them to look for explanations that go beyond the obvious. The rewards are huge. Remind them: Once your partner has stated an idea, it cannot be changed. (See **For the Players** above.)

groups of 4+

Freeze Tag Forward-Reverse

For the Emcee/Teacher: This is a fun version of Freeze Tag for five advanced players. One player performs a scene alone (about any topic she chooses) until one of the other players calls out "Freeze." The first player then freezes in place and the other player comes onstage and uses the frozen position to create a new two-player scene. One by one, each of the five players freezes the game and joins the group onstage to begin a new, larger scene until all are onstage (going from the one-player scene up to a five-player scene). By this time, five completely different scenes should have been played out onstage.

Now freeze the whole thing and make the players do the scenes again, this time in reverse order. The player who created the current five-player scene must find an excuse to exit the stage. Once that player leaves, the scene instantly goes back to the four-player scene that came before it. This continues until the original player is alone again, finishing her original scene.

For the Players: When you create your scene, give the other players something to work with. Try not to choose a scene that is too similar to the one before it—don't freeze a dance scene and change it to an aerobic workout. Don't keep a player stuck in the same position in every scene. Just because a player is curled up as a stump in one scene, you don't have to cast him as a rock in the next scene. He might contribute more to your scene as an astronaut, and part of the fun will come from watching him justify his strange position.

When the scenes reverse, remember that the change is instantaneous: Whatever pose you find yourself in at the end of one scene, you have to use for the beginning of the next scene. If you are on the ground when the scene switches, but you're supposed to be a tree in the next scene, you can't suddenly stand up. Instead you have to explain why you are on the ground.

Before leaving a scene, try to put the players in positions that will be fun for the audience. One of my personal favorites is to come into a scene as a drill sergeant. Right before I leave, I make the players do push-ups. Then it's up to them to explain why they are doing push-ups in the next scene.

Action Figures

For the Emcee/Teacher: In this game, as in many improv games, two players act out a scene based on a situation or setting suggested by the audience. But there's a twist: The players are fully poseable "action figures." They can't move by themselves, but they can talk. Two other players (the controllers) must move the action figures into poses. The object for the action figures is to verbally justify the positions that they are placed in as they act out the scene. The action figures should retain any position they are put into. To make the figures walk, the controllers can tug at their pants legs or give a light kick to the backs of their feet.

Variation: In a performance situation, this game also works well as an audience participation game. Call up two audience members to be the controllers who pose the action figures.

For the Players: As an action figure, always keep in mind not only your own position, but the other action figure's position as well. You need to know what he is doing so that you can justify your position relative to his.

Even though your movements are being determined by the controller, you are not helpless. You can still take command. If you want to reach for something, just say so and the controller will help you do it. Do the same thing if you want to walk somewhere. Soon you will discover that you are the one in charge, and you and your partner can still do a scene. On the flip side, if the controller has put you in a strange position, go with it. The audience will love the fact that you did.

Lastly, be aware that this scene will almost always end with a fight or a hug. I'm not sure why that's the case, it just happens—sort of like death and taxes.

Tips for Teaching: This is a great game for teaching students about body positioning. It is up to them to justify their changing positions. Get them used to being led around. Have them switch between being an action figure and being the controller. Also, remind students that they can give clues to the controller about what they'd like to do ("I'm going to start running away now," for example).

Bionic Parts

For the Emcee/Teacher: This game was inspired by the 1970s television shows "Six Million Dollar Man" and "Bionic Woman," in which the heroes had super "bionic" body parts that were scientifically enhanced. Call a group of players onstage to play a team of superheroes. With the help of the audience, assign each member of the team a bionic body part—maybe a nose that can smell for miles, or a supersonic double-jointed elbow. Then give the team a problem that they need to solve using the assigned body parts.

For the Players: Find out which team member has a plan. Once the plan is in motion, go with it. This is a physical game. If your body part has a moving joint, really go for it: make your movements big. This game is perfect for performers who like to do physical comedy.

Tips for Teaching: We tend to think of our body as a whole, and overlook the potential of isolated movements. This game lets players focus on one small part of the body and make it seem very important. Encourage players to see how much they can do with their bionic parts. At the same time, make sure players work together as a team to accomplish their mission. This game helps them see the big picture and the details at the same time.

small group

Discworld

For the Emcee/Teacher: Invite a group of players to perform a scene about an everyday situation chosen by the audience. Explain that they will be performing this scene on an (imaginary) unsteady platform that is perfectly balanced on the head of a pin. This means that if the players don't keep themselves evenly distributed around the center of the stage, the platform could fall. If too many people are on one side of the stage, someone has to move. The catch is that players can't just move: they have to have a reason to move that's related to the scene. (The scene they are performing should be completely unrelated to the Discworld setting.) For instance, if the players are kids on a playground and everyone has gathered on one side of the stage to look at a bug, two of the players might get mad and go off to the other side of the stage to play by themselves. Players must justify every move they make.

For the Players: Use your body to help create the illusion that the "platform" is tilting whenever you are out of place. In Quick Wits, the actors who are not playing a game sit onstage, and they help keep up the illusion as well. The audience will be keeping track of where everyone is, so be careful: They'll notice if you are out of balance. It is fun, however, to knowingly be wrong and then have to fix it.

Tips for Teaching: This game is designed to show the effect of "countering" as a blocking technique. (Countering is moving across the stage to fill the space left by another actor's movement.) Playing the game should help students understand how one movement can lead to another movement. The hardest part of this game for students is trying to maintain the scene as they play. Remind them to keep the scene going and justify their movements.

Improv
Olympics

For the Emcee/Teacher: The audience suggests a basic household chore or occupation and players present it as if it were an Olympic event. Two players should be the commentators for the event. They set the scene by describing the competition and introducing the other players, who play the contestants, a coach, or whatever may be needed. Make sure it is clear to everyone what type of competition this is going to be: Is it a race? Is it a test of strength? Is it synchronized?

For the Players: Several gimmicks work well in this game. The most common is having a tragedy take place during the event, and watching the athletes overcome it. For instance, in a synchronized dishwashing competition, one athlete might accidentally drop a plate, which smashes on her foot causing her pain, forcing her teammate to pretend to drop a plate on his foot and hop around faking pain to match his partner. Often the commentators will review some of the event using slow motion. This works well and gives the audience a chance to see "what went wrong." You can also use judges' scoring and interviews with the athletes afterwards if the skit needs an extra push.

Tips for Teaching: Students who are familiar with sports television will have an easier time with this game. Encourage the athletes and sportscasters to work together to shape the event. Give them a few seconds before starting to decide as a group what type of event they want to run (power, speed, synchronized). You can adapt the game for younger students by playing the commentator yourself.

groups of 3

Stand Up, Sit Down, Bend Over

Props: one or more chairs

For the Emcee/Teacher: The rules to the game are in the title. As three players perform a scene, at all times one player must be standing, one must be sitting, and one must be bent over. If one player changes position, the others have to change too. Whenever players change their positions, they

have to justify the action with reasons related to the scene. Before players begin, ask the audience to suggest a setting for the scene; a location where action can take place, such as a construction site.

For the Players: The idea is to work together, so don't change your position if the other players can't see you. You may make them look silly, but the audience will think that your team can't pull off the game. It helps if you can say something to announce your move. If you are standing, you might let the other players know you plan to bend over by saying, "Look, a penny on the ground." You can even just say straight out that you're going to sit down. Once you've played the game for a while and the audience sees you can do it, make it go wild. Start making moves quickly as the scene is ending. Here's a fun gimmick: Two players are in the same position (both standing, for example). They both try to correct it by moving, but choose the same position again (perhaps both bent over). If this keeps happening, the audience will love it.

Tips for Teaching: Remind students that they must let the other players know when they are going to change position. They can make sure the others are watching them, or give a verbal cue, such as "It's time for my yoga stretches."

Stunt Double

For the Emcee/Teacher: Invite two players onstage and have the audience suggest an everyday activity for them to do in a scene, perhaps cleaning the house. The players should silently think up lots of reasons why that everyday activity is extremely dangerous (for example, a monster in the closet, a man-eating vacuum, exploding socks in the drawer, etc.). Explain that because this task is so dangerous, the players have hired a professional Hollywood stunt person (the third player) to do all the hard parts. Players set up the dangerous aspect ("I want to clean the refrigerator, but I just remembered that I put a 600-pound Bengal tiger in there") and then they call out, "Stunt double!" This signals the stunt double to come onstage and act out the dangerous task. When the stunt double is done, she leaves. Then the other players come back on as if they survived the ordeal easily, and, in true Hollywood fashion, take all the credit.

For the Players: This game is obviously very physical. The stunt double should be someone who can express a lot with her body. The other players have to set up the stunt double with fun bits to do, but they must be careful not to put in too much. It still has to be something that she can act out. Here is a fun gimmick that can be used every once and a while: after players set up the task, the stunt double can come in and do it with ease. An example could be: "Oh, no, the box in the closet is next to a bomb that could go off when it is moved!... Stunt Double!" The stunt double then just moves the box without incident and tosses it to the other players as if it was no big deal.

Tips for Teaching: Inexperienced players tend to give the stunt double too much to do. Encourage them to make the activities simple enough to act out. The stunt double will need to use mime skills to make the scene as believable as possible.

groups
of 3

Helping Hands

Props: table, supplies for a messy project (see below)

For the Emcee/Teacher: Set up a table onstage with supplies for a messy project, such as decorating a cake, folding a paper airplane, or bandaging a wound. Invite three players onstage to act out a scene in which a player performs this project. However, this player (the "body player") does not use his own hands to do the project. Instead, the body player puts his arms behind his back. Another player (the "hands player") stands behind him and puts her arms through the body player's bent elbows, creating the illusion that the hands player's arms belong to the body player's body. The two players must work together to maintain this illusion. The body player must justify what the hands are doing. The reverse is also true: if the body starts talking about something, the hand gestures need to match this. The third player (the straight man) is the person the task is being done for—the bride whose cake is being decorated, the kid who wants a paper airplane, or the wounded patient.

Variation: An audience member could play the "straight man" in this scene.

For the Players: This is a great, messy game. Have fun with it. If you are the body player, act as if you are in complete control, even though "your" hands are doing all sorts of strange things. If you are the hands player, make sure your hands are always expressive. Big motions will give the body player something to work with. The straight man is often forgotten in this scene, but he doesn't need to be. He is there as a foil, and can set up funny bits for the body and hands players to do. Often he is the target for the messy aspect of the scene. The audience loves the silliness of this game.

Basic Scenes

Now the emphasis is on putting together a real scene. The games in this section all have a bit of silliness in them (that's what makes them fun to do), but the goal of every game is to develop a full scene.

To build a scene, the players have to keep in mind that each scene should have a beginning, a middle, and an end. Scenes shouldn't just stop; they have to reach some kind of resolution. Remind players to remain true to each character they create and stay with it throughout the scene. Players are allowed to have fun, but encourage them to keep the goal (building a scene) in sight at all times.

Photo by Bob Bedore

32

Animal Soap Opera

For the Emcee/Teacher: Invite a group of players onstage to act out a typical soap opera scene, with tragic events, forbidden romance, unlikely coincidences, and, above all, overacting. But this is a soap with a difference: All the players will be a particular animal. For example, players might present a scene with an evil twin being acted out by hamsters. Have the audience suggest the animal and a situation or setting for the scene.

For the Players: Work as a team to get in all the animal stereotypes you can, while keeping a soap plot going. It is helpful to create a list in your head of everything that relates to the animal. A hamster "hitting the bottle" is funny because we know that hamsters have the little water bottle hanging upside down in their cage. Keep the animal first in your mind, the soap plot second. When it comes to the soap opera side, remember that overacting is the key.

Between the Lines

Props: two very different scripts (or other reading materials, such as flyers, magazines, even menus)

For the Emcee/Teacher: Invite three players onstage to perform a scene about a particular topic or situation, suggested by the audience. Give two of the players different scripts or other reading materials. These players will speak only lines they find in these reading materials, picking whatever they want from the text on the page. Meanwhile, the third player (the middleman), who has no script at all, has to make up dialog so that the scene makes sense. His job is to justify and incorporate the other players' scripted lines into the topic the group has been given for their scene.

For example, let's say two players (Tim and Tammy) are reading from different scripts, while the middleman (Dave) is making up the dialog. The setting for the scene is Summer Camp.

Dave: This is the spot. Let's set up camp.

Tammy: This is a most deplorable situation, Big Momma.

Dave: I don't care if you like the spot, this is where we are setting up camp. And stop calling me Big Momma.

Tim: I know who the murderer is!!

Dave: That's great, but let's save the ghost stories for later, around the campfire. Speaking of which, why don't you go get some firewood?

Tammy: I don't touch the stuff.

Dave: All right, how about you?

Tim: He used a Butter Knife!

Dave: Well, I'd use a saw, but whatever works for you.

The scene can continue from there. Dave will need to create the plot for the story and guide the scene to a resolution.

For the Players: As always, listening is very important in this game. For the readers it is important to scan the pages as quickly as possible so that you have an idea of the types of lines your script includes. This will let you work promising lines into the scene. Also, keep in mind that you don't have to read everything written. If you see a line that is a paragraph long, but the third sentence is the only part you want, just read the third sentence. Don't read more than you need. The key for the middleman is to respond to what is going on and then get it to flow with the situation. Don't spend time acting as if the other person is crazy (even though it will sound like that). Try to make it work.

Tips for Teaching: Often students will think that the reading parts are not exciting, because they are not improvising. Remind them that they have to choose which lines they will read, quickly scanning the script to find things to say as the scene goes on. This actually makes the reader's job even harder than the job of the middleman, who can make up whatever she wants to say.

small
group

First Line,
Last Line

For the Emcee/Teacher: Bring a group of players onstage to perform a scene. Ask the audience to give them the first and last lines of the scene, as well as a setting. Players can do anything they want in the scene, as long as they begin and end with the correct lines.

For the Players: You don't have to worry about rules in the middle of the scene, so have fun with it until you are ready to wrap it up. Decide among yourselves who is going to deliver the final line, to help make the dialog flow smoothly. Stretch the game out a little, and don't rush to the last line. If possible, don't make the train of thought too obvious. The audience will want to see you struggle to reach the final line. You might even tease the audience—say the beginning of the line to make them think you are coming to the end, but then change the line and take the scene in a whole new direction. When you finally do get around to the last line, it will be even more satisfying to the audience.

35

small
group

Oscar-Winning Moment

For the Emcee/Teacher: Have a group of players perform scenes from a (made-up) Hollywood blockbuster that has been nominated for several Academy Awards. (Ask the audience to suggest a title for the movie.) Stop the movie periodically to call out "Oscar-Winning Moment!" Name a player and the category of the nomination (Best Actor, Best Special Effects, Best Original Song, Best Sound Editing, Best

Documentary, and so on). The player you named should then step up and show why she's Oscar-worthy. If the nomination is for acting, the player should go all out and overact. Think, for example, of the "I Never Learned to Read" scene from the movie *Wayne's World*. Players should be prepared to perform any category: They might morph into a monster for Best Special Effects, somehow transform what they are wearing for Best Costumes, or sing the Best Original Song. But don't throw in too many strange award categories that are difficult to act out. "Lifetime Achievement" won't do anything to further the scene.

For the Players: This is one of my personal favorites. Really let loose and have fun with the scene. Don't just act—*overact*! Make sure that your "moment" makes sense in the scene, while at the same time taking it to a new level. Most moments are going to fit into one of two categories, tear-jerker or inspirational. Often the moment is both.

pairs

Pieces
of Paper

Props: about six slips of paper with lines of dialog written on them

For the Emcee/Teacher: This is a popular game with both players and audiences. In advance, cut about six slips of paper and write a line of dialog on each one, such as "You're just a big squeezy bear." Fold the slips, scatter them across the stage, and ask two players to perform a scene. (Before they begin, ask the audience to supply a setting or situation for the scene.) As the scene goes on, players have to reach down every once in a while and pick up a piece of paper. Players should open the paper and read it aloud as their next line of dialog. Tell players that they must make each line of dialog fit into the scene they are performing. They should explain why they said what they did, or justify the line with their actions. The scene continues until all the pieces of paper are gone.

For the Players: The most important part of the game is setting up the pieces of paper. Each paper has a line of dialog written on it, but you won't know anything about the subject matter until you read it aloud. The simplest way to treat the papers is to set them up as quotes. Your setup should be something like this: "I've got one thing to say to you, and it is...," "Do you know what she said to me? She said...," "That sign clearly says...," and so on. Don't set up a piece of paper with something like "I think that you are a...." As you can see, that's not going to lead to a quote.

Be careful not to throw too many twists into your scene, or the pieces of paper won't have as much impact. Let the papers provide you with the twists. Performers love this game because each piece of paper is usually a laugh in itself, so they feel confident playing the game for an audience.

Fairy Tale News

For the Emcee/Teacher: Give a group of players a fairy tale or nursery rhyme to act out as if it were a breaking news story on television. The audience can suggest the fairy tale or nursery rhyme. One player should be the news anchor, another is an expert brought in by the station to give her insight, and the third player is the reporter at the scene. The reporter should interview various witnesses or characters involved in the event, portrayed by the other players. (One player can act out all of the interviewees, if you are working with a small group.)

For the Players: The real key to this game is to take the events of the fairy tale or nursery rhyme and make it seem logical that this is a news story. A story on "Jack and Jill" could start with: "Tragedy at the hill today as two local youths tumbled. One is suffering a broken crown." Make it seem as much as possible like an actual newscast, because it's the incongruity between the format and the subject matter that will really sell the skit. Watch the news and see how the anchors handle reporters in the field. The people being interviewed by the reporter don't all have to be central figures in the fairy tale. Maybe the interviewees are only people who witnessed the event (like Little Red Ridinghood's nosy neighbor), or people who once dated the central character or taught him in elementary school. As players, try to take a second to plan the parts you will play before beginning.

groups of 4+

38

Fairy Tale Courtroom

For the Emcee/Teacher: Have players act out a courtroom drama based on a nursery rhyme or fairy tale chosen by the audience. One player (or emcee, or audience member) is the judge. One player is the prosecutor, one player is the defense attorney, and the rest play the witnesses. (One player can portray all the witnesses, if you are playing this game with a small group.) Encourage players to play the scene straight, as a serious legal drama: that will make the fairy tale elements even funnier.

For the Players: Look for elements in the fairy tale that work in a courtroom. It's easy to see what the wolf would be accused of, but what about the little pigs? Make the scene look like a serious trial, but incorporate all the wacky elements you can, and everything will fall into place. Think of bizarre witnesses you can bring in. Talk to the audience as if they are the jury. Turn the fairy tale and the courtroom upside down.

Talking Columns

For the Emcee/Teacher: This is an audience participation game, but in a classroom situation players can take the role of audience members. Ask the audience to suggest a setting or situation for players to act out in a scene. Invite two members of the audience onstage and have them stand at opposite sides of the stage. Ask the audience members to help the players by making up lines for them. Whenever a player touches one of the audience members (they are the "columns"), the column should tell the player what word or words to say next. The players then must make the lines fit into the scene and justify why they said these things. This game is similar to Pieces of Paper (Game #36), except that the lines come from audience members instead of paper slips.

For the Players: As actors, make sure that you are letting a real scene develop. Don't go to the columns too often at first; let them get used to being a part of the skit. Begin by giving the columns obvious choices. You might say something like, "I can't believe you filled my shoes with _____," and then touch the column to fill in the blank. This gives them a chance to get a feel for the game. Watch out for audience members who are difficult to work with—some might respond too slowly or decide to say inappropriate things. If necessary, take a difficult audience member out of the game by simply staying away from him.

Variation: Use one of your columns to change the character's emotion instead of giving lines. See Emotional Scenes (Game #17).

groups
of 3

Ask the Prompter

For the Emcee/Teacher: This game has much in common with Talking Columns (Game 39). Invite an audience member onstage (in a classroom situation, use a player). Explain that two actors will be practicing a scene, and the audience member is to help out by being their prompter—the person who follows along with a script and reads the actors their lines whenever they forget them. Unfortunately, the play's script has been lost, so the prompter will have to say the lines "from memory." Have two players perform a scene about a topic chosen by the audience, acting as if they are in a really bad community theater production. Every once in a while, the players should stop and call out "line," and the prompter must give them their next line. The prompter can also tell the actors when their blocking is wrong, "reading out" the correct stage directions.

For the Players: Don't ask for lines too often, especially at first. Keep it simple until the prompter starts to get a feel for the game. Always be sure to justify the prompter's lines, making them fit into the scene.

Character Games

These games give players a chance to develop some fun characters. Some of the games structure the characters for players, but others allow players to be completely free.

Characters are important to improv, and players should learn how to create them. I like to spend plenty of time working on characters with the students in my classes. Each student creates a character whose identity is the complete opposite of the student's real-life identity. Then I have students interview each other in character, and write stories about the characters they interviewed. It's a fun exercise that puts the players and their characters to the test.

The most important rule of any game involving characters is that each player must stay in character throughout the entire scene. The audience will not appreciate an actor who is not remaining true to the character.

Animal Police

For the Emcee/Teacher: This is a strange little game that some love and some hate. Ask the audience to choose a familiar animal (such as a dog, cat, or monkey), and invite two or three players to portray a humanized version of that animal. The animals live in a house and have jobs and so on, but their animal nature influences everything they do. For example, the dogs might work as paleontologists (digging up bones), and the mice probably have a big wheel in their exercise room. Explain that this type of animal has been outlawed by the local authorities. Have two or three more players be the Animal Police, who have come to the house searching for the illegal type of animal. The animals try to hide what they are, while the police try to discover the truth. The police ask questions, and the animals try to answer them without giving themselves away.

For the Players: The police need to be more "bad cop" than "good cop." They need to intimidate the animals. Still, make sure the police don't dominate the skit—the animals should get their moments to shine as well. The animals really have to play up the stereotypes to make this work. Their house should seem exactly like a human version of this animal's habitat. If you are playing a police officer, make up questions by thinking about the animal's habits and what that animal might own. For example, the Animal Police could question the "dogs" about why they have movies like *101 Dalmatians* and *Lassie Come Home* in their video collection. The police might ask the "cats" why they have a big pile of sand on the bathroom floor. The animals will have to make up good excuses. As in Animal Soap Opera (Game #32), it is helpful to keep a list in your head of everything related to your animal.

Bad Advice

For the Emcee/Teacher: Bring three players onstage to give the audience (or other players) advice. Each player creates a quirky character who shouldn't be giving advice to anyone. The characters introduce themselves and explain why they want to give advice to people. Let's say they decide to be a video game enthusiast, a survival expert, and an obsessive librarian. Invite questions from the audience, and choose a few to ask to the players. Choose basic questions, so that the players have room for freedom in their answers.

For example, someone might ask: "My boyfriend has been giving me hints that he wants to date other people. What do I do to keep him?" The obsessive librarian might say, "Well, I could tell you the answer, but I think you would find it a lot more rewarding if you found it yourself. I suggest a tour of your local library. Maybe a few minutes in the reference section will give you what you need." Then the video enthusiast might chime in: "I would suggest leaving the room and then coming back. I find that whenever I've messed up on something, if I just leave and come back, it's as if nothing happened. But once you've got him hooked, you'd better save the game right there. That way you can always come back to that point." Finally, the survival expert says, "Can you find his food supply? Because if you can, I'd just take a bit of metal shavings and put them in the food supply. You won't have to worry about your little boyfriend anymore." Now just ask another question and continue.

For the Players: Make sure you come up with a character whose voice you feel comfortable using to answer questions, and stay in character. Don't choose a one-joke character—unless you can answer every question with that one joke. Find out what characters the other players have chosen, so that you don't have two similar characters. The more bizarre the character, the better. "The evil clone of Mark Twain," created by actor Russ Peacock, is one great example. Don't limit yourself to answering questions; the real fun begins when the characters start arguing about what the other characters have said.

Characters
and Objectives

For the Emcee/Teacher: Bring a group of players onstage and give each of them a very different type of character to play. One might be a used car salesman, another a pirate, another an astronaut, and so on. Then give the group a problem that they must overcome or a goal that they must accomplish as a group (such as ending world hunger). They have to use their individual talents to make it happen. Ask the audience to supply both the problem and the character types.

For the Players: Be the character, but don't try to be normal—exaggerate your characterization. At the same time, work with the other players. Watch what they are doing and interact with them to develop a scene. The interest lies in seeing the characters doing activities they wouldn't ordinarily be involved in.

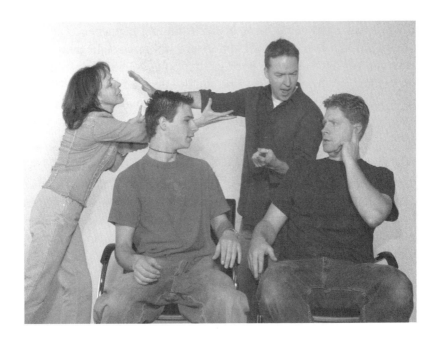

Old Job/ New Job

For the Emcee/Teacher: Ask the audience to suggest two jobs. Two players will pretend to be workers doing one of the jobs. Then bring another player onstage to be their new coworker. This third player used to work at the other job, and keeps working this new job the way he worked the old one. An example might be a man who used to be a fry cook now having to be a construction worker.

For the Players: The third player needs to take charge of the scene. It's as if the character thinks she knows exactly the best way to work this new job, even though she doesn't and is just relying on her training at the old job to get by. The other two players are basically straight men—they should help set up funny bits for the third player.

Here He Comes Now

For the Emcee/Teacher: This Character Game has a bizarre twist: One player's character is created by other players, who describe the character before he comes onstage. As the scene begins, two coworkers (players one and two) are talking about another employee. They bring up all the personality traits that really bug them about the character. The coworkers might describe traits and quirks like these: "He always talks with his hands," "She does the worst Michael Jackson impersonation, but thinks it's really good," or "Every time he hears his name he does a summersault and goes, 'ta-da!' " Finally they say, "Here he comes now." At this point the character (player three) has to enter and act out all the negative attributes the other players gave him. We usually give the character about four traits to work with before calling him out. As the emcee, be ready to end the game before it wears out its welcome. After the character comes in, the game will only last about a minute before it starts to get old.

For the Players: If you are one of the coworkers describing the character, it is your job to set the scene. Establish a workplace setting—you might be on the job or at the water cooler. Make it clear that you are gossiping about someone who works with you. As for the quirks you describe, give the character good material to work with, but don't describe things she can't do, like a back flip. Otherwise, you'll just make her look bad. Remember the Golden Rule and don't give the character bits that you would not want to do yourself. Give at least one of the quirks a trigger, such as "She cries whenever we talk about cats." This makes it simple to work the quirk into the scene.

You have a tough role if you are the character, because you'll be given some strange things to do. When you are offstage, really concentrate on what the coworkers say. Pay special attention to the triggers, because the audience will be looking for them and will notice if you miss them. The key is just to have fun with the characterization. Really play up annoying characteristics, prompting your coworkers to recoil from your actions.

Nightmare Auditions

For the Emcee/Teacher: Like Here He Comes Now (Game #45), this game forces players to act out bits chosen by another player. Have the audience choose the title of an imaginary movie or play. Then choose a player (or two) to portray a director holding auditions for this movie or play. She calls in hopeful actors (the other players) to audition one by one. Each actor introduces himself in character, and then the director tells him what she wants him to do. She might choose something simple: "Do the scene where the lead professes her love" or "I want to see the death scene." The director can also make it harder: "Sing a song from the musical portion" or "I've heard you wrote a poem about why you want to be in this show. Why don't you read it to me now?" The game is in the hands of the director. If she suddenly says, "I've got it! We need William Shatner for this part. Get him here to audition now," the next player will have to do a Shatner impression. She can also tell an actor to do the scene again, but in a different way (perhaps as a worm). This game is really fun for actors who have gone through a lot of auditions in their lives or for young actors who have just endured their first one.

For the Players: If you are the director, keep in mind that you might have to play the actor someday, and you don't want revenge hanging over you. Don't give players bits they can't do. Try to keep in character and keep the scene flowing. Let players come out more than once, to audition as different actors. This gives them the chance to try out a variety of characters, and also gives you a chance to make players do funny bits. If you are one of the actors, it's important to listen for what the director wants you to do. (Wow, it's just like real life!) Do whatever you can to fulfill the director's wishes; remember, you want this part. Have fun choosing very different "actor" characters for each turn you take auditioning.

Teamwork

Teamwork is important in almost any improv game, but, as the title suggests, these games rely on teamwork even more than usual improv games. They are all group efforts, and can't possibly be controlled by one person.

In a class, use these games to help players learn to rely on others when necessary, and to be reliable themselves when other players need them. These games thrive on give and take, which is crucial to improv.

Photo by Bob Bedore

groups of 4

Double Date

For the Emcee/Teacher: This game lets two players meld to become one character. In One-Word Story (Game #8), players took turns adding one word each to a story. In this game, pairs of players talk as a team, switching back and forth on words. For example, to say the phrase "Hi, how are you?" a pair would alternate like this: Player one says "Hi," player two says "How," player one says "are," and player two says "you." The pair of players should speak like one person with two heads.

Now comes the really hard part: bring two pairs of players onstage and have them hold a conversation talking this way. Each pair plays one character in a scene. Ask the audience to supply a simple situation for the scene, such as a blind date.

For the Players: Work as a team. Listen to what is being said, because sometimes you may think that the conversation is going in one direction when it is really going in another. The audience will love it if you don't pause too much between words. Make it sound like a real conversation, and don't forget to act. You are not robots. Show emotions and move around the stage as you would in an ordinary scene. Try not to stand in place, or this will become a static "talking heads" scene.

The Oracle

For the Emcee/Teacher: Line up three or four players one behind the other, facing the audience at center stage. The player in the back of the line should stand up tall, the player in front of him should duck down a little so that the back player's face can be seen, the next player should duck down a little more so that the player behind her can be seen, and so on to the player at the front of the line, who should duck lowest. Now you have heads on top of heads, like a totem pole. This is the Oracle, and it can answer any question asked of it.

Invite questions from the audience and relay them to the oracle. The oracle should answer the questions in the style of One-Word Story (Game #8), with each player adding one word to the answer until it is done.

For the Players: Listen carefully to the question that is asked and try to make sure your response answers the question in some way. Use your arms to give the Oracle the feeling of being a larger-than-life mystical creature. Move your arms when speaking and then drop them when you are finished. This not only looks cool, it also lets the audience know when you're done with a question.

Soap Interpreter

For the Emcee/Teacher: Have a group of players perform a scene from a soap opera while another player is off to one side interpreting the scene for the "comedically impaired." Choose a good physical comedian to play the interpreter. The interpreter is really just doing a quick charade for each word or phrase; she is not trying to do real sign language. The audience can suggest a setting or topic for the scene.

Variation: This game can be played as a talk show instead of a soap opera.

For the Players: If you are the interpreter, focus on the words being spoken onstage. Don't get caught up in the scene as a whole, just the words. You can choose whether to act out each word individually, or pantomime the whole sentence. For the Players acting out the scene, the key is to work with the interpreter. Be sure not to talk too fast. You must let the interpreter do his bit, since he's the real comedy factor in the game. The interpreter needs to be able to hear—and perform—each word or phrase separately, so don't overwhelm him with an extremely long sentence. Set the interpreter up by using words and phrases that are fun to pantomime, such as "you could have knocked me over with a feather" or "that was hard to swallow." If you see that the interpreter is having a hard time with a word, don't keep using it.

If the skit is not going well, there are a few gimmicks you can use to bring it to a satisfying ending. One is to give the interpreter a very physical pantomime to do—"falling," for example. Then make her do it over and over. Another gimmick is to find good phrases like "role model" that will give the interpreter a fun bit to wrap up with (rolling on the ground and then modeling).

Speak As One

For the Emcee/Teacher: Line up a group of no more than five play-ers onstage. Have them gather close together in a slight semicircle. These players all represent one character, and must speak all together in one voice. This character will be an expert on a topic the audience suggests (dog catching, for instance). Ask the character entertaining questions about the topic, and then have the group answer your ques-tions as one.

This game is fun for audiences, because they can sense how hard it is to speak with one voice. It's funny when players make a guess about what the group will say next and speak the wrong word out loud. This game shows players (and audiences) what it's like for a group to think on their feet all together.

For the Players: It's always best to make your line a bit of a semicir-cle. This way the players can see each other and get an idea of who is leading the answer. Don't start talking until you know that the other players are with you. To keep the group together, you may want to agree beforehand on a word or phrase that you will always say before you actually answer the question. This will get all of you on the same rhythm. It works to give a slow "Well," to start everything. You can also repeat the question. If the emcee asks you what the best part of being a dog catcher is, you can start by saying, "Well, the best part of being a dog catcher is..." and then answer.

groups
of 4+

Spelling Bee

For the Emcee/Teacher: Two teams compete in a strange spelling bee. Each team chooses one character type for all the members to portray—perhaps everyone is a cheerleader. Invite the audience to suggest an extremely difficult word for one of the teams to spell. The whole team will work together to spell the word: The first team member calls out one letter, then the next calls out another letter, and so on until they reach the end of the word. This is similar to One-Word Story (Game #8), except the players call out single letters instead of words. Players should call out the letters as quickly as possible, so they will probably not spell the word correctly. Then the team speaks in unison, defining the word and using it in a sentence. For more on speaking in unison, see Speak As One (Game #50). The teams take turns spelling words for a few rounds. End the game with a bonus round, in which each team creates a new nonsense word by adding random letters one at a time. Write the new word on a chalkboard or easel as the team creates it. Then have them speak in unison to pronounce the word, define it, and use it in a sentence.

One of the funny parts of this game is the characterization. For example, a cheerleader spelling-bee team might stand with their arms linked and have big smiles on their faces. The emcee gives them the word *fragmentation*. They take a deep breath and shout all together, "Ready?! Go! Fragmentation!" Then they begin to spell the word one letter at a time. Each team member might say, "Give me an—" before his letter. Then the team says the word again in unison and ends with a cheer. Teams can choose any type of character. Pirates would be really good at using the letter *R* ("arrgh"). Vampires might hiss or say "Blah" before each letter. Astronauts might give the illusion of floating in space while they are saying their letters. It's up to the players.

For the Players: Speak the letters quickly so that the crowd can't really be sure what you are spelling. Since you're spelling so fast, the word may be badly misspelled, but act as if you did it perfectly. When you are coming up with a new word, make sure you include a few vowels. Listen to the letters that come before yours and choose a vowel if necessary. You're not trying to form an actual word, but you do want to be able to pronounce it. One fun gimmick is to add umlauts, hyphens, and so on as you spell the word.

52

Triple Dub

For the Emcee/Teacher: This game is a real mindbender for the players. It was inspired by "dubbed" foreign movies, in which we see one actor on screen but hear the voice of another actor speaking the lines. Triple Dub complicates the situation even further: Three players are onstage, acting out a scene. Each of them acts the part of a character, but speaks one of the other actor's lines. For example, Andrew might speak for Jon, while Jon speaks for Becca, while Becca speaks for Andrew. The player who is speaking covers his mouth loosely with one hand, while the player whose lines are being dubbed mouths the words as well as she can to make it seem as if she is the one speaking. The players can make each other do lots of strange and funny things by dubbing lines, and make the audience laugh at the same time.

For example, Becca might put these words into Andrew's mouth: "May I have this dance?" Andrew will have to mouth the words and step forward invitingly, but if he doesn't want to dance he might dub this line for Jon: "Sorry, I can't dance: I have two left feet." This game takes a lot of practice because you have to keep two characters in your head at once: You need to match your actions to the lines being put in your mouth and, at the same time, come up with lines to dub for your target player.

Variation: You can adapt this game for beginning players by having three offstage players dub all the lines for the three players onstage.

For the Players: This game forces you to be constantly on your toes. While you are trying to think of something for your target player to say, another player may be dubbing your lines. Always remember who has your "voice," so that you don't miss any lines they speak for you. When you dub lines for your target player, speak in a strong voice, so that the player can act out what you are saying. Place your hand over your mouth to make it clear (to both the players and the audience) that you are not speaking for yourself. While keeping track of all this, make sure to develop the characters' relationships and motivations so that the scene can progress. Lastly, try not to overlook blocking (see page 23): Make sure that you don't just stand there.

Singing Games

Singing games are perhaps the hardest of all improv games to play, but they also provide the greatest rewards. The audience will go nuts when a Singing Game is played well, and they don't get too down when it's only so-so, because they know how hard it is—and so will you.

Trying to sing while doing improv is like walking and chewing gum and saying the alphabet backwards and working on a hard math problem and memorizing Shakespeare, all at the same time. Not only are you trying to come up with rhyming words that make sense, but you also have to keep it all in tune. It's the ultimate challenge in improv.

When you are trying to improvise song lyrics, the best advice I can give is to create a list in your head of all the words that have to do with your given topic. If you have time, create a second list of words that rhyme with every word on the first list. Here's another hint: I like to think of my rhyming scheme backwards. I work out how the line will end first, and then go back to work on the beginning. It gives me a light at the end of the tunnel to move toward.

53

Blues Song

Props: live musical accompaniment (optional)

For the Emcee/Teacher: This is a rhyming song game. Blues is a musical style well suited to improv, because blues songs often have little musical intervals between each line of lyrics. These intervals give players a pause to make up the words. Give a group of players an audience-suggested topic for a blues song, and have them take turns singing lines. The first player sings an opening line, and the next player must follow that with a line that rhymes. The third player starts a new line, and the fourth player must rhyme it. The players keep taking turns until the song reaches a satisfying ending. In between each solo line of lyrics, all the players should sing a wordless bluesy melody together. A song might go something like this:

Player one: I had a good friend and his name was Jay.

Everyone: Boom, ba ba, Doom, ba ba, doom ba doo.

Player two: He never really had all that much to say.

Everyone: Boom, ba ba, Doom, ba ba, doom ba doo.

Player three: But he went to the store to pick up some bread.

Everyone: Boom, ba ba, Doom, ba ba, doom ba doo.

Player four: And that's when he saw a sight that filled him with dread.

Variation: This game can be played with other musical styles (such as country or rap) as well.

For the Players: Listening is especially important in this game for two reasons. First of all, you have to listen to the story that is taking shape in the song, and second, you must know what word you'll need to rhyme. Work together to build the song. Concentrate on your phrasing so that it flows with the other players' singing styles. Remember that you only have one line, so you won't be able to create your own story. Just go with the narrative that the whole group is putting together. If you are singing the first line of a rhyming couplet, you may feel tempted to choose words that are hard (or impossible) for the next player to rhyme, but try not to do this. Remember that you're working as a team. There is one exception: If you have played the game together many times, and you know the next player is excellent at making rhymes, try throwing him a curve.

Da Doo Run Run

Props: live musical accompaniment (optional)

For the Emcee/Teacher: This musical rhyming game is set to the tune of the familiar song, "Da Doo Run Run." The audience should suggest a one-syllable name (Steve, for instance) to rhyme in the song. As in Blues Song (Game #53), players take turns adding lines to the song. If you are familiar with the original song, you know that there are three rhymes close together. In Quick Wits, we give all three to one player. It really impresses the audience if the three rhymes all work together. This is an elimination game: If a player can't think of a word, she is out; if a player uses a word that has already been used, he is out; and if a player makes a rhyme with a nonsense word, she is out. After completing one verse successfully, players should go on to the next verse, still rhyming the same name. The song goes down the line until only one player is left standing.

> Player one: Met him on a Monday and his name was Steve
>
> Everyone: Da Doo Run Run Run, Da Doo Run Run
>
> Player two: As soon as I saw him I had to leave
>
> Everyone: Da Doo Run Run Run, Da Doo Run Run. Da Doo, Da Doo, Yeah
>
> Player three: He made me believe
>
> Everyone: Da Doo, Da Doo, Yeah
>
> Player three: There was nothing up his sleeve
>
> Everyone: Da Doo, Da Doo, Yeah
>
> Player three: But he lied and I did grieve
>
> Everyone: Da Doo Run Run Run, Da Doo Run Run

For the Players: Just keep in a groove, and have a lot of rhymes ready. If you only have one rhyme, the person just before you is guaranteed to choose the same word. Don't forget to try rhyming the word by just taking away the first letter ("us" for "Russ").

small group

Gibberish Opera

Props: live musical accompaniment (optional)

For the Emcee/Teacher: Invite a group of players to sing an opera in the great foreign language of Gibberish. Players will sing nonsense words in operatic style while using gestures and blocking to act out a drama. In some ways this game is easier than the other singing games, because the players don't have to rhyme all the time. Still, the lack of words makes it challenging to keep a story moving. Ask the audience for a situation to act out in the opera, and be sure to choose a simple one. Then let the players take it away.

For the Players: Make the plot extremely simple and easy to follow. Remember to use big expressions, gestures, and movements to convey the story as you sing. The opera spoof will be more fun if you use all the opera stereotypes you can. Using lots of vibrato and holding out high notes for long periods of time will help. Remember that operas aren't just solo arias; the characters should interact and sing "duets."

Musical
Between the Lines

Props: live musical accompaniment (optional), two very different pieces of reading material (scripts, magazines, books, dictionaries, etc.)

For the Emcee/Teacher: This game uses the basic format of Between the Lines (Game #33), but adds music and takes out the middleman. Have a musical improviser provide the accompaniment for two players singing a duet. The players find the lyrics for their duet in the text of a book, magazine, or other piece of reading material. Give each player a very different text to sing from.

Variation: Instead of singing a duet, the two players can be soloist and backup singer.

For the Players: Don't sing over each other. Try to scan your reading material while the emcee is talking so that you have an idea of what lines might be used. You can choose any text you want from the material, and use only as much as you need. As with any singing game, take the time to get the feel of the music before you start singing. It might be best to sing short lines at first so that the pacing of the music won't throw you off. As you play more you can start adding longer lines.

Object of Desire

Props: live musical accompaniment in pop ballad style (optional)

For the Emcee/Teacher: Ask the audience to suggest an inanimate object. Now have a player sing a love song to the object. The player must make up the lyrics on the spot. This is a simple concept to be sure, but also one that can be tricky to pull off.

For the Players: Think of the object and why someone would love it. I know it may not be easy to love a hairball (which is one I've had to sing about), but you can make it work. (I sang the love song from the point of view of a cat.) To make coming up with lyrics easier, keep a mental list of everything related to that object. Keep in mind that this is a ballad—the slow nature of the song will help you put it all together.

groups
of 3

Three-Headed Monster

Props: live musical accompaniment (optional)

For the Emcee/Teacher: Invite three players to stand together and become a monster with three heads. Now have the monster sing a song. As in Double Date (Game #47), each head can say only one word at a time. The three players should take turns singing the song, each adding one word at a time. For example, the monster would sing "I love you" as follows: Player one: "I," player two: "love," player three: "you." Ask the audience to supply the song's topic.

For the Players: Remember that you can only sing one word at a time. Pay attention to what the other players are singing and try to make the song flow. It's hard, but try to work in rhymes. The audience will love it. You might work in a rhyming chorus that you can keep going back to between verses. Because it repeats, the chorus will be easy to sing well.

On Your Toes

The games in this section force players to pay attention, because something new is happening every few seconds. This type of game is my favorite kind of game to play.

The section begins with "call games." In a call game, the emcee calls out changes as the scene goes on, and players must react instantly. I believe that doing improv means having to empty your mind as quickly as possible and then refill it with whatever you are given. Call games force you to empty and refill constantly as the scene moves along, and there is something really magical about that.

The directed games at the end of the section keep players on their toes by making them follow the direction of the emcee, the way an orchestra follows a conductor. For these games to work, the emcee must be in tune with the players, so that she can cue each player at just the right time. It takes a little practice to get this right, but the practice really pays off when the games are played for an audience.

Photo by Bob Bedore

59

Silly Accents

For the Emcee/Teacher: Ask the audience to suggest a topic for a scene and have players act it out. Meanwhile, you will be calling out various accents (Scottish, Italian, Southern, Klingon, etc.) every fifteen seconds or so. The players have to switch their accents instantly. This is a call game like Emotional Scenes (Game #17), but much harder.

For the Players: One word—stereotypes! This game is all about stereotypes. For a fake accent to be recognizable in only fifteen seconds, it has to be a caricature; think Inspector Clouseau. It's not just the accent; it's the way you hold your body, your tone of voice, your whole character.

The other trick you can use to make an accent more convincing is to mention details about the region where the accent originates. Even if you can't do an authentic English accent, you can talk about afternoon tea, the queen, and the like and survive for a short time. One night we were playing this game with a first date as the topic, and the emcee called out Dutch as one of the accents. I couldn't really think of the accent at the time, so I just said, "Well, I paid for my half." The line got a huge laugh.

It is important to listen for the emcee to call out accents. If you don't know an accent the emcee calls, let another player speak. If no one onstage knows the accent, just fake it until the emcee changes it. Don't be afraid to change the scene as it goes along. Let the accent take the scene where it might need to go, but remember that there is still a central theme to work with.

Film and TV Styles

For the Emcee/Teacher: This game allows players to display their whole range of acting talents, from martial arts to Shakespearean tragedy, all in one five-minute skit. As in Emotional Scenes (Game #17) and Silly Accents (Game #59), players act out a scene while you call out changes. This time players switch to different acting styles. These acting styles can come from different types of theater, or from any film or TV genre (Action, Situation Comedy, Medical Drama, Tennessee Williams play, and so on). The players have to switch instantly when a new style is called out, just as in the other games. Ask the audience to suggest styles before you begin, and try to use as many different ones as you can. Also have the audience supply a situation for players to act out in the scene.

For the Players: Hit the stereotype of each style, because you won't have enough time to develop anything subtle. Let the styles guide the scene, but make sure you keep the narrative thread continuous. Be ready for anything. If you are performing for an audience, listen to the audience when the emcee invites them to shout out suggestions. The emcee will use a lot of these, so if you hear any off-the-wall suggestions (Kabuki, for example), think about what you could do if you suddenly had to switch to that style.

Occupations

For the Emcee/Teacher: This game combines the quick changes of call games like Silly Accents (Game #59) with the body positions of Freeze Tag (Game #23). Ask the audience to suggest lots of occupations. Choose an occupation that involves movement, and have two players act out workers doing that job. As the scene goes on, call out different jobs for the players to act out. No matter what their position, players must instantly switch to the new job. They will have to justify why they would be in those positions, using reasons that make sense with the new job. For instance, players might be coal miners digging, and then switch to fashion models. They could explain that they are bending over to adjust their designer shoes.

For the Players: Using your body is very important in this game. The emcee will not be able to call a new job if you're just standing there, so do something. The real joke in this game comes from being in a strange position when a job is called that would never put you in that position. Work as a team and see who has the best idea to justify the position so that it makes sense with the new job. Keep up the energy throughout the scene.

small group

Shopping Mall

For the Emcee/Teacher: Like Occupations (Game #61), this game combines elements of freeze games with the call game format. Have players begin acting a scene set in a typical mall store—either a specific chain store or a type of store. As the scene goes on, call out the names of other stores. The players are instantly transported to the new store, no matter what position they are in or what they are about to buy. Before you begin, have the audience suggest stores to include.

For the Players: Big body positions will be the key in this game. Anything you can do to set up a change in location will help you and the emcee work together. You might hold up some huge item so that the emcee can switch you to a store that sells smaller items, like a candy shop. Putting yourself in an embarrassing position and then being transported to another store will give you something to work with. A good gimmick is to buy something odd or embarrassing; when the scene changes, you'll have to explain why you're holding the item. Going from Victoria's Secret to Radio Shack could be fun.

groups
of 4

Four Ways to Die

For the Emcee/Teacher: The format of this game is different from the others in this section, but it shares the element of quick, constant change. Ask the audience for four different ways that a person can die (drowning, devoured by wild boars, boredom, etc.) and a setting for a scene. Now have four players act out a scene in that setting. During the course of the scene, each player must die in one of the four ways suggested. The tricky part is that none of the players knows how the others will die, so players may find that the death they had planned has already been done. It becomes harder and harder for each player to make her death work in the context of the scene, especially if players wait too long and the easy ones are gone.

For the Players: Keep listening to see what the other players are setting up. They might give a hint about what type of death they are going for. But watch out—some players will sound as if they plan to die in one way, only to switch to a different death at the last moment.

Even with all the deaths happening around you, remember that you are still acting out a scene. You have to justify each death by acknowledging it and making it work in the context of the scene. The last player not only has to justify the deaths and come up with one of her own, but she also has to end the scene by herself. It's tough, but it's also fun.

Lie Detector

Props: buzzer and bell (optional)

For the Emcee/Teacher: Invite three players to come onstage. Have two players act out a scene about a topic chosen by the audience. The third player will be a human lie detector, and must monitor the scene for falsehoods. The lie detector will make a buzzer sound whenever she sees or hears something that might be untrue. The players onstage must then change the action or phrase until the lie detector gives them a "ding" to let them know they have it right.

For example, let's say the scene is about baseball. One player is the coach and calls in a baseball player: "Simmons, get in here!" The player comes in, running. The lie detector buzzes him: "Buzz." The player must do his entrance again, and this time he rolls in. Lie detector: "Buzz." The player again goes out and comes back in skipping. This time the lie detector gives a "Ding!" The coach justifies the skipping: "Good work, I see you're doing those drills I've been teaching. Now look, I want to move you to a different position. I want you to play pitcher." Lie detector: "Buzz." Coach: "I want you to play catcher." Lie detector: "Buzz." Coach: "I want you to play the organ during the seventh inning stretch." Lie detector: "Ding!"

For the Players: If you are the lie detector, be careful not to overdo the buzzer. Let the scene develop between buzzes, because the changes will take the scene in new directions. Each time you decide to buzz, try buzzing twice (see the example above), to give the player a chance to come up with something really fun. Here's a good gimmick for the players in the scene: When you are buzzed you can either do the exact opposite of what you just did or do a variation of it. This will give you time to think of something else to do (usually something very, very bizarre) on the next buzz.

Another gimmick is for the lie detector to ding before the player says something. For example, the player says: "I'm a man." Lie detector: "Buzz." Player: "I'm a woman." Lie detector: "Buzz." Player: "I'm a..." Lie detector: "Ding!" Then the players just shrug and go on with the scene.

Fiendish Torture

Props: bells, whistles, and other noisemakers

For the Emcee/Teacher: This is an audience participation game. Have a group of players perform a scene while the audience plays a very evil part. Choose a different trigger sound, such as a bell or whistle, for each player, and give the triggers to audience members. Give each player something physical he has to do whenever his trigger is heard. This could be something like somersaulting or acting like a chicken. Ask the audience for a topic or setting, begin the scene, and invite the audience members to sound their triggers whenever they want.

For the Players: Don't miss a trigger or the audience will be unhappy. This game is for them, so do your best and have fun. Honestly, there will never be much of a scene because the triggers will be coming fast and furious. Just try as hard as you can to make the scene work while still responding to every trigger.

small group

Superheroes

Props: alarm sound effect (optional)

For the Emcee/Teacher: Ask the audience to suggest an imaginary world-threatening crisis. Players will be a group of superheroes who must save the world from this crisis. Have one player begin the scene alone, and ask the audience to supply her with a special power. This player acts out her character until the alarm sounds (usually only a few seconds). She becomes aware of the crisis and calls for help from the other heroes, who come onstage one by one. When the next player arrives, the first player greets him by his superhero name. The name should indicate the hero's special power, such as Rubber Cement Man or the Human Fax Machine. The player must instantly become that hero, with whatever powers that name might imply. Each hero is introduced by the hero that came onstage just before him. This continues until all are onstage; then they combine their powers to solve the crisis.

For the Players: Making up a silly superhero name for another player is fun, but don't make up something that is impossible to act out. Remember that you are working as a team, not fighting each other. Still, your names can be just about anything: The Woman Who Only Speaks in One-Word Sentences, Madonna Boy, Man With No Bones, and so on.

Make sure that every hero has her chance to shine. Don't act over the others too much. Give the audience a chance to see each hero and keep in mind that you still have a crisis to overcome.

Barnyard Symphony

For the Emcee/Teacher: In this game, you are the conductor of an animal orchestra. Have players stand in a line and give each one a different animal to play, as suggested by the audience. Whenever you point to a player, he must make the sound of his animal. Like a conductor, you can use your other hand to adjust the sound: Move your palm up in a big, expansive gesture to mean louder; move your palm down in a smaller, inward gesture to mean softer. Hold your hand open to sustain the sound, or cut it short by closing your fingertips together. The idea is to create a little musical number featuring the sounds of the players' favorite animals.

Variations:

- Assign an emotion to each player, instead of an animal. Whenever you point to a player, she should make a sound expressing that emotion: a cry of sadness, a roar of anger, and so on. Players will find that it's easy to express some emotions in sounds, and harder to express others. Tell them to just try their best with the hard ones.

- Combine the games so that you have emotional animals to work with. Imagine a symphony composed of a neurotic chicken, an angry cow, and other such animals.

For the Players: The emcee may point to more than one animal at once, so be ready to go for it. Make sure that your animal's sound is distinctive and recognizable. On the other hand, try to keep in mind that the noises are supposed to create a type of song. Just as in a choir, try to blend. Choose an animal sound that you can make several times without hurting your voice.

Genre Bending

For the Emcee/Teacher: This game is somewhat similar to Emotional Storytelling (Game #20), but without the emotions. Give players a familiar story to tell, such as a fairy tale. Then assign a different literary or movie genre (western, sci-fi, horror, Dickens novel) to each player. As players tell parts of the story, each will tell it in the style of his genre. Players should stand side by side. Have one player begin telling the story. Each of the other players should be ready to take over the story in a different genre as soon as you point to them. The audience can suggest both the familiar story and the different genres.

For the Players: Keep in the spirit of the genre assigned to you. If you are telling the story in the style of a western, talk in a drawl and include lots of livestock. If you are telling it in sci-fi style, change the livestock to robots, and so on. At the same time, keep the general thread of the story going; it should still seem like the same story, just in a different style. You have to be listening the whole time so that when the emcee points to you, you can run with it. I suggest keeping an eye on the emcee, because emcees often look at the player they are about to choose just before pointing. If the emcee looks your way, be prepared. Sometimes with a game like this you can find a phrase to say or a bit to do (like just letting out a big scream for "horror") whenever the finger points to you. This can be extremely funny, because the emcee will know what to expect when coming to you and can work you in at just the right times.

Guessing Games

Guessing games work well onstage for one simple reason: The audience already knows what the players are trying to guess, so for the first time they feel as if they are ahead of the players. They have a great time watching players squirm while trying to guess whatever it is they've picked out for them.

There are two main types of guessing games in improv, one with verbal clues, the other with physical clues (charades). Both are fun to play, and this book includes examples of both.

The best way to teach players these games is to play charades a few times. Once players have some practice with basic charades, it will be easier to incorporate charades and guessing into the context of a scene.

Idiot Poker

Props: paper and pen, tape

For the Emcee/Teacher: This game is based on the card game, in which each player has a card attached to his forehead—everyone else can see what the player's card is, but it is a mystery to him. Send three players out of earshot and have the audience choose personality traits or character types for them. Write the characters or traits on pieces of paper, call the players back in, and tape the papers to their foreheads. Each player can see who the others are, but no one knows what is written on their own paper. Give the players a topic for a scene and have them act it out while trying to figure out their identities.

The players should give each other clues about who they are. For example, in a scene about making a cake, one player might have the secret identity of Cleopatra. The other players might say something like, "No wonder you can't make this cake. You're always in De-Nile."

For the Players: Play the scene big. Going overboard will help make this game a lot of fun for the audience. Your job is to treat the other players exactly as you would treat someone who possesses the secret character type or personality trait listed on their card. At the same time, you have to pay attention to the way the other players treat you, and listen for any hints they might drop. Once you know who you are, show the other players you have guessed, so that they can stop giving you clues. You want every player to guess correctly, so look to see who is having trouble. Never come right out and tell players who or what they are. Try to get the point across in a subtler way, using clues.

Late for Work

For the Emcee/Teacher: You'll need three players for this game. One player acts the part of a person who is always late for work, one plays the boss who wants to fire him, and the third player is the coworker who wants her buddy to keep his job. Before the scene starts, send the player who is late for work out of earshot. Ask the audience to suggest a place where the characters work, and then ask for three reasons why the person is late. Start with a basic reason (for example, he couldn't find the keys), then choose a slightly more bizarre reason (a truck full of pogo sticks crashed on the freeway), and then go for something really big (ninja penguins hijacked his car). As an emcee you can lead the audience to give you stranger reasons, or simply say something like, "He was walking along and something fell out of the sky and landed on him. What was it?"

Bring the player who is late back in and begin the scene. The player must make excuses to his boss, but they must be the three excuses supplied by the audience. As the boss grills the player on why he is late, the coworker stands behind the boss's back and tries to help her buddy get the answers right. The coworker can only use charades to convey the correct excuses to her buddy.

For the Players: Make sure you keep in mind where you're working—use this in the skit. Just be sure you don't put in too much detail and drag out the skit. If you are playing the boss, you can add to the fun by turning around, catching the coworker in strange positions. Listen to the audience and you will know when the coworker is doing something really wild. The coworker will then have to justify the position, somehow making it plausible within the work environment. Beware, however, not to use this gimmick too much. If you do, the fun will wear off and the skit will become too long, because turning around interrupts the charades. For the other two players, keep the basic conventions of charades in mind. Tugging your earlobe for "sounds like" can be extremely useful. As the late worker, if you guess the excuse right away, feel free to give a "fake" guess first. This is hard to do without looking fake, so be careful.

Murder Mystery

For the Emcee/Teacher: Begin with a group of four or more players and send all but one of them out of earshot. Ask the audience to give the one remaining player a location for a murder, the occupation of the victim, and the object that was used as the murder weapon (think LOW—Location, Occupation, Weapon). Now call a second player to join the first onstage. The first player must convey the details of the crime to the second player, using only gibberish and charades. Once the second player thinks he understands everything, he should use the correct object to "kill" the first player. Each of the remaining players comes onstage one by one, silently guessing the items and killing off the preceding player. By the end of the game, there should be a pile of bodies on the stage. The last surviving player should then announce her guesses for the three items. If she misses any, have the preceding players announce their guesses to see if anyone got it right.

For the Players: When you are doing the charades, help the player who is trying to guess. If you try something a few times and the player doesn't get it, try something different. Keep looking for other ways to get your point across. When you are guessing, be sure of each item before moving on to the next one. You can confirm your guess by doing a little charade back to the other player to show what you think the answer is. Big actions will help make the game funny. Stick with the improv motto and go for the stereotypes—use any murder mystery clichés possible.

72

 groups of 4

News Quirks

Props: desk and chairs for newscasters (optional)

For the Emcee/Teacher: Players will act out a television newscast in a fun Guessing Game. Choose players to be the news anchor, co-anchor, meteorologist, and sportscaster. Send the news anchor out of earshot and ask the audience for odd quirks—obsessions, minor problems, other jobs, and so on—that the other players will have to act out while they serve as co-anchor or report on the weather and sports. Throughout the newscast the anchor tries to figure out the other players' quirks, announcing her guesses at the end.

For the Players: As the anchor you are in control. Always remember that this is a newscast, and conduct it with dignity. It is not your job to shout out guesses during the skit. If a player finishes his segment and you are still unsure of his quirk, you can do a follow-up story or special report later in the newscast. This will give you another chance to guess. Announce your guesses at the end by saying something like, "Well that's the news for now. For my co-anchor, a little boy lost in the mall; my meteorologist, who has an obsession for dry erase markers; and my sports anchor, who thinks he is in a Jane Austen novel, I'm Wendell Combover saying good night."

As for the three other players: Go overboard with your quirks, but still do your job with the newscast. If the anchor comes back to you a second time, she probably has not guessed your quirk, so make sure that you give an easier clue. Of course, she may just go back to you because what you did was so funny she feels the audience would like a little more.

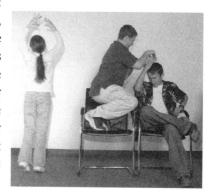

groups of 4

Party Quirks

Props: doorbell sound effect (optional)

For the Emcee/Teacher: This is News Quirks (Game #72) moved to a party format. As in News Quirks, send one player out of earshot while the audience suggests quirks (bizarre character traits) for the other three players, who will all play guests at a party. Maybe one guest thinks she's trapped in a video game, and another is obsessed with lint. Bring the first player back in and have him play the party's host. He begins the scene alone by preparing for the party for a few seconds before you ring a doorbell sound effect. Then the first guest enters and acts out her bizarre quirk. The guests then enter one by one, announced by the doorbell, as the host tries his best to guess their quirks.

For the Players: The most important difference between this game and News Quirks is that the host has less control than the anchor. The anchor decides the order of the different segments in the newscast and can return to players whenever she wants, but in Party Quirks the emcee decides when the guests will arrive. The other difference is that the host guesses the quirks during the skit instead of at the end. Still, remember that you can't just stand around and make guesses; you have to keep the skit moving in a party format. You can incorporate guesses into the skit by introducing one guest to another: "Have you met the woman who thinks she's trapped in a video game?" for example. Make the party convincing. Tell the audience what type of party you are hosting and make sure that you keep the environment believable throughout.

As a guest, you need to make your characterization big. Since the host's guesses are the point of the game, you should help each other out. If you can see that the host has no idea what another guest's quirk is, step in and give some hints—just stay in your character.

Plea
for Help

For the Emcee/Teacher: Bring a pair of players onstage. One is a foreign dignitary, sent from his country to the United Nations to ask for help in a crisis. Some people do not speak the dignitary's language (Gibberish), so a UN interpreter (the other player) will be translating the dignitary's speech. (The interpreter doesn't even understand the language herself, but she will fake it so that she can keep her job.) Send the interpreter out of earshot and ask the audience to suggest the crisis facing the dignitary's country (for instance, Smurfs are threatening war). Bring the interpreter back in and have the dignitary make his speech to the UN (the audience). The interpreter must translate the speech correctly. The foreign dignitary can use gestures and charades to give the clues that the interpreter will need to guess the nature of the crisis.

Variation: You might decide to have two dignitaries instead of one, to make acting out the crisis easier.

For the Players: Both the dignitary and the interpreter have to keep going, so there is not much rest in the game. If you are the dignitary, keep up the act of pleading desperately with the UN, when what you are really doing is giving hints to the interpreter. As the interpreter, the key is to keep talking while you watch for clues from the dignitary. Even though you will probably make several wrong guesses, pretend that you are doing a good job of interpreting.

pairs

The Return Department

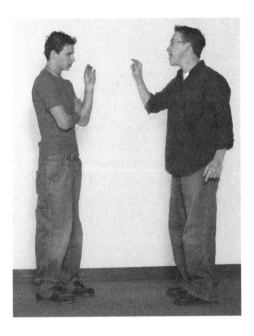

For the Emcee/Teacher: You need two players, one to play a store clerk and one to play an unsatisfied customer. Send the customer out of earshot and ask the audience to suggest a product that a person might return to a store because it is defective. Now bring the customer back onstage and begin the scene. The customer is bringing the product back to the Return Department. The clerk at the Return Department asks the customer to explain how the product is defective. This will be difficult, because the player acting the customer doesn't know what product the audience chose. The clerk asks the customer questions about the product, giving the customer subtle clues about what it is. Finally, the customer is able to name the item he wants to return, and the clerk gladly takes it back.

For example, perhaps the product is a set of dentures. The clerk asks the customer to explain the problem. Although he doesn't know what the product is, the customer must come up with a reason why it is defective. Perhaps he says something like: "The 'On' switch doesn't make it go." This puzzles the clerk: "Uh, sir, I don't think you want them to be electric"—a slight clue. Customer: "No, of course not. But that's not the only problem. They're also the wrong color." Clerk: "What color were you hoping for, sir?" Customer: "Red." Clerk: "I'm afraid we discontinued the red; our customers were accused of vampirism." Customer: "Well, what colors do you have?" Clerk: "White, off-white, and smoker's taupe." At Quick Wits any player would have figured it out by now, but would draw out the game with problems and uses completely unsuited to dentures.

For the Players: As the customer, don't think too much before answering the first few questions about the product. Just give an answer. Not knowing what the product is usually leads to some unintentionally funny answers. Give demonstrations or tell embarrassing stories of what happened when it didn't work: Feel free to say things like, "It didn't work right when I sat on it," because you don't know what it is, and sitting on it might be a pretty funny thing to do. As the store clerk, wait a few questions before asking any questions that contain hints. That way the customer has an opportunity to give funny, incongruous answers.

What Am I Doing Here?

For the Emcee/Teacher: Bring up three players and send one (the guesser) out of earshot. Have the audience help you put together a list of three common, everyday activities (like riding a bike). Then make them not so common (I'm riding a bike, but instead of a seat I'm sitting on a _____). The audience fills in the blank (let's say, with "cactus"). Bring the guesser back in. The other players must help the guesser guess each activity using only gibberish and mime skills. The guesser must say all the elements (I'm riding a bike, but instead of a seat, it has a cactus) to receive full credit.

Variation: This game is even more fun when two teams of three compete against each other and the clock. Each team has a minute and a half to try to guess all three activities. Teams earn three points for each one they get right. If they get all three in time, they get an extra point. Should a guesser be stumped, the other team has a chance to steal for one point. The guesser should raise her arm when she thinks she has the answer, so that the emcee can stop the clock.

For the Players: Just be fast. Make sure the guesser knows what's going on (riding a bike) before you go on to the strange part (the seat is now a cactus). Establish the ordinary and then mime taking it away and replacing it with something strange. One effective way to do this is to pretend to throw the item that is being replaced (the bike seat) off the stage. That way the guesser knows exactly what is being swapped out.

Narrative Games

A narrator plays a central role in each of these games. Playing the narrator is one of the hardest jobs in improv. The narrator has to take a scene from beginning to end, while still letting the other players have their moments to shine.

The directions for the individual games provide some tips for the narrator, but it will still take some practice to get the timing right. Players who want to work on narration can learn a lot from watching television shows that are narrated by a host. The narrator's disembodied voice speaks throughout the show, though the narrator is seldom seen. This is the feeling players should go for.

Some of the games might be tougher for younger players because the narrator's role is so challenging. In this case, the teacher may want to handle this type of role until the students are more comfortable.

Fairy Taled

For the Emcee/Teacher: This game takes a fairy tale and shows what happens after the "happily ever after" ending. Have the audience choose a fairy tale. Maybe Cinderella finds out that Prince Charming has already married Snow White, or perhaps Hansel and Gretel eat the witch after putting her in the oven. Players must act out a sequel for the well-known story. The easiest way to make this work is for a narrator to pretend to read the sequel while the other players act out what is being read. Although the narrator is in control of the scene, she should still give the other players freedom to make up their own lines and actions.

For the Players: You've got all the ready-made characters to work with, so don't forget to use them. Now you just have to think of something bizarre in the "ever after" to make the scene work. The narrator "reading the book" needs to be a confident, talkative improviser. However, you can play the game by just acting out the story without narration. That's the beauty of improv—if an aspect doesn't work for you, change it.

small group

Behind the Fairy Tale

For the Emcee/Teacher: Ask the audience to suggest a fairy tale, and have players explore "behind the scenes" of the story we all know and love. This game parodies the cable television channel VH1 and their *Behind the Music* series. (Each episode is a documentary about a rock star or band, often documenting high times, internal tensions, and bad behavior. The structure usually follows the group's rise and fall, sometimes with a comeback at the end. I'd suggest watching a few episodes before trying this game.)

Give the players a fairy tale to work with and send one player to the side to act as narrator. The narrator talks about what really happened behind the scenes of the familiar fairy tale. The other players are the characters in the fairy tale and act out whatever is called for by the narrator.

Let's use the example of "The Three Little Pigs." The narrator might begin the scene like this: "The Three Little Pigs. Sure, we all know the story, but until now no one knew that there was a deeper

Photo by Bob Bedore

story going on.... Behind the scenes, all was not as it seemed in the Pig home." Now the players act out a scene: Perhaps the mother pig finally puts her foot (hoof) down and kicks out her three sons, who have been living at her house too long. The narrator introduces a new scene: "So off they went, but why didn't the brothers stick together?" Players might speak directly to the audience for this scene, as if being interviewed for a documentary. We might find out that two of the brothers hate the other one—possibly because "he always hogs the best stuff" (like the bricks). The narrator might introduce an interview with the wolf, who is upset about being treated like a villain: "I'm a wolf; eating pigs is what I do. Do I look at you like you're a sick person because you eat doughnuts?!" The sketch goes on in this vein until it reaches some sort of resolution. In this case the brothers might put aside their differences to save their lives.

For the Players: Everyone knows these characters, but in this game it works well to play them a little differently. Think about the Big Bad Wolf as a Woody Allen type, or Sleeping Beauty as a chain smoker. Now you're starting to get somewhere.

The ending to this game is probably the hardest part. It's best to make it tie in with the original ending of the fairy tale; that way everyone knows where the story is going. Perhaps the characters all put aside their squabbles to make sure the fairy tale would end well, and no one was ever the wiser...until now.

small group

"A&E Biography"

For the Emcee/Teacher: This game is inspired by the cable channel A&E and its popular "Biography" series. This show profiles celebrities and historical figures, always including a few reenactments of episodes in the subjects' lives. Ask the audience to suggest a celebrity, either real (like Bill Gates) or fictitious (like Captain Hook). Have one player be the host. The host talks about the celebrity's life and introduces reenactments of key episodes, which other players act out. These episodes should start out simple and become stranger and stranger.

The narrator might begin: "Welcome to 'A&E Biography.'" Tonight we will look at the life of one of our most beloved entertainers—Barney the Dinosaur. Life didn't start out full of love for this mega-star. In fact, it started out cruelly." Now the players act out this harsh beginning. Maybe Barney was never loved as a child and no one would hug him. Maybe he was teased for being a purple dinosaur. When the brief reenactment ends, the narrator speaks again. "Barney tried desperately to fit in and took some odd jobs to help out." The scene goes back to Barney, working, perhaps as a fast-food cook. "But all that was forgotten one day when Barney met someone who changed his life." The players act out what happened. Was the someone a television producer? The person who taught him to love? It's improv, so anything goes.

For the Players: The host begins by setting up the other team members with easy situations to act out. The situations can move on to the bizarre as the skit grows. For the other players, the key is listening to the host. She usually starts with the celebrity's childhood and progresses from there. Make sure you know what characters the host is introducing and what situation they are being put in. Make your reenactments short and to the point. Don't draw out the reenactments; if the skit needs more, the host can just move on to another point in the subject's life.

Tips for Teaching: The game is easier for students if they are familiar with this type of TV show. If necessary, describe the show to them or show them short clips. It is best to play this game with fictional characters at first; that way the students aren't trying to recreate actual events. You can adapt the game for younger students by playing the narrator yourself.

small group

Coming Attractions

For the Emcee/Teacher: Ask the audience to suggest an ordinary, everyday activity. Have a group of players use this everyday activity as the basis for the preview or trailer for a new action movie. Imagine the new action blockbuster, *Taking Out the Garbage!* One player will be the announcer, while the others act out what the audience would see on the screen.

For the Players: As the announcer, try to sound like the stereotypical movie preview. Use phrases like "The action event of the summer," or "Action has a new name and it is. . . ." Introduce the actors with names that sound like stage names for action movie stars, such as Rock Hardbody or Lance Starcatcher.

For the actors in the movie, the key is to make a normal activity (like taking out the garbage) look like a death-defying feat. Work together to get the most out of the scene. Throw in special effects if you can—slow motion always works. If possible, try to work in plot twists, like a love triangle or a musical number, to give the preview some spice.

Tips for Teaching: Before playing the game, have students discuss movie previews and what they are like. Help them identify some of the clichés and commonly used devices of previews. They can use the information from the discussion to help them play the game. You can adapt the game for younger students by playing the announcer yourself.

Playing Creator

Props: microphone (optional)

For the Emcee/Teacher: Choose one player to be the Creator, an all-powerful deity who created the world on the stage, and can change it at will. The other players will be people living in the Creator's world. The Creator will talk over the microphone, changing the world from time to time, and the other players should act as if they don't know they are being controlled by the Creator. At random times the Creator can ask the audience how they would like the world to be. The weather can suddenly change, or aliens can invade—whatever the Creator and the audience want to see.

For the Players: As the Creator, you have full control, but don't misuse your power by making changes constantly. Give the other players a bit of time to react to each change before doing something else. If you are one of the other players, try to help the Creator find good bits to do. For instance, you might pick up a flower, knowing that the Creator will then do something to that flower. As a player in the Creator's world, you need to work within the environment. Just go with it.

Paperback Writer

For the Emcee/Teacher: This game lets the audience watch a brilliant novelist at work. Choose one player to be a writer, and invite the audience to choose the genre or style of her next book—perhaps a noir thriller, a Hemingway novel, or a mass-market romance. The writer sits at a "computer" and narrates as she types out the manuscript. The other players enter one by one as the writer introduces each character in the novel. They act out everything as it is being written. The writer should let the other players come up with their own dialog and limit herself to narration.

For example, given the genre of Romance/Science Fiction, the writer mimes typing on a keyboard. She narrates what she is typing: "The two moons and four suns of Balen Prime IV were shining brightly as the young space ranger stepped from his ship." We see a player stride across the stage like an astronaut in zero gravity. "It took him a moment to realize that he was not in zero gravity." The player now walks normally. "The pull of gravity was close to Earth's, but not quite the same. Actually, it made him much heavier." The player walks with great effort. "Then his eyes spied the loveliest sight he'd ever seen." Another player enters with a sexy walk. The writer says to herself, "No, I don't like that, too early for the love interest." She now hits the backspace button, deleting what she's written, and the second player walks backwards as if being pulled away. As the scene continues, the writer can let the players do their own talking by simply saying, "The space ranger took one look and said...." And if she doesn't like what the players say, she can always erase it and try again. It's fun when a player says something strange, or garbles his words, because the writer can just say something like, "Spell check should have caught that."

For the Players: As a character in the novel, be careful not to take the scene away from the writer. Let the writer give you things to do and then work with those ideas. As the writer, try to make the narration sound like a book. The gimmicks in this game are simple to pull off: The writer can erase anything he thinks is not working and rewrite that part of the story. Every once in a while, the characters can mispronounce words in the dialog, and the writer can do a spell check to get the word right. The writer can make the characters do some strange things, or say lines in a bizarre way, by just typing this into the story.

Tips for Teaching: You can adapt the game for younger students by playing the writer yourself.

groups
of 4+

Slideshow

For the Emcee/Teacher: Ask the audience to name two kinds of animals. Players will combine these two animals into one (for example, a porcupine and a hamster could turn into a "porcuster"). They will introduce this previously unknown species to the world in a low-budget public access cable television show. Two players are the hosts of the show and talk about the animal. They show slides that they took of the animal in the wild. These "slides" are actually freezes performed by the other players. The hosts then have to describe what is being shown, keeping in mind that they are talking about this new animal.

For the Players: If you are one of the players in the slides, make your positions wild to give the hosts good material to work with. As one of the hosts, when you try to describe a slide, the first thought that comes to mind is usually the best. Don't spend too much time looking

at the slide without talking. You can use a couple of gimmicks to help this game work. The best one is to say that the "slide" being shown is upside down. This forces the players to try to form the picture again, but flipped. It's a cheap stunt, but it always works. You can vary the format a bit by saying you have video footage of a scene. As hosts, be enthusiastic and full of energy, but not polished or TV-savvy.

History Bluffs

For the Emcee/Teacher: Ask the audience to name a common household appliance (like a toaster) and a historical event (the signing of the Declaration of Independence, for example). Tell them it's a little known fact that the household appliance the audience chose actually came about because of that very historical event. Choose one player to be the host of a television show telling the story of how the appliance and the event are linked. The other players will reenact key scenes introduced by the host. The format of this game is similar to that of "A&E Biography" (Game #79).

For the Players: Keep the reenactments short and follow what the narrator is saying. The key is to make the link between the appliance and the event seem plausible. Here's a good gimmick: Foreshadow the invention by describing the exact workings of the device, but dismiss it as an impossible dream. You might say something like, "Boy, this bread is cold. If only I could come up with a device that would hold the bread in a metal cabinet while thin coils were heated up all around the bread after a lever is pushed down. Then, after just the right amount of time, the bread would pop up toasted perfectly on each side. But I guess that will never happen." The scene should end with the narrator saying something like, "And that's how the (event) brought about the item we now know and love, the (invention)."

Tips for Teaching: This game works better when the narrator knows something about the historical event, so try to select an event your students are familiar with. Still, if all else fails, just have players make everything up. Remember, it's fake history anyway. It's great to watch students imagine how something like the Civil War might give rise to the invention of the computer.

Mind Games

These games all use language in unusual ways. To pull them off, you have to have a unique mindset. I'd like to say you have to be more intellectual, but that isn't always the case. Sometimes "smart" players have trouble with these games, while the players you least expect may excel.

When playing these games for an audience, it's helpful to keep up with the news. Throwing in topical subjects always works well, because the audience recognizes the joke and immediately gets the connection. It also doesn't hurt to make the audience think that you're a well-rounded person.

Some of these games might be a little more difficult for the younger players to grasp at first, but in my experience they start to pick them up after a few tries. Just don't give up on your players and they won't give up on you.

Dr. Seuss

For the Emcee/Teacher: Have the audience suggest a historical event. Players will present this event as it might have happened if the children's author Dr. Seuss had written the story. (Dr. Seuss was the author of such wildly popular books as *The Cat in the Hat* and *Green Eggs and Ham*, all written in rhyming verse.) This should be more than a read-aloud—encourage players to act out a fully dramatized scene, with blocking and dialog. The only difference will be that the dialog is in "Seuss-speak."

For the Players: Rhyme. Rhyme. Rhyme. Try to make everything you say sound like a Dr. Seuss book. Don't forget that Dr. Seuss made up many of the words in his books. If you are stuck for a rhyme, just make up a nonsense word that rhymes. Words like "flibberflabbets" will really add a Seuss flair to the scene. At the same time, remember to keep the scene flowing.

Tips for Teaching: To introduce students to Dr. Seuss (or refresh their memories), have them read some of his books aloud before beginning. Point out the strong rhythm of the lines, the frequent rhymes, and the nonsense words.

Questions? Anyone?

For the Emcee/Teacher: Have two players act out a dialog in which everything they say must be phrased as a question. Does it sound simple? Have you tried it? You'd be surprised how difficult it can be. Whenever players accidentally respond with a statement instead of a question, they are out. Replace them and keep playing. Have the audience supply a setting or situation for the dialog.

For the Players: Don't just answer questions with questions. Try to make your dialog tell a story. The death of this game is boring dialog like: "Why are you here?" "Why are YOU here?" "Didn't I ask you first?" "Didn't I ask you second?" Make it fun. Here's an example of a good exchange set in a department store: "Can you help me?" "Don't you see the name tag that says, 'I can help you'?" "Does this shirt come in other colors?" "What color are you looking for?" "Does it come in orange?" "Is the Pope Catholic?" "Why don't you have any of the orange shirts out here?" "Haven't you heard about the ring of orange shirt thieves in this mall?" "Are they dangerous?" "Do you consider harpoons dangerous?" and so on.

As you can see in the dialog above, rhetorical questions can be used to mean yes or no ("Is the Pope Catholic?"). You can make up fun rhetorical questions, too, like "Is Vanna White?" or "Is Deborah Harry?" If you use the right enthusiastic or sarcastic tone, the meaning will be obvious.

Short Attention-Span Theater (SAS)

For the Emcee/Teacher: The pace of this game is quick, because players must take turns speaking short lines. Ask the audience for a situation or setting. Have players act out a scene, but tell them they can speak only in three word sentences. Once a player has said his three words, he must wait for another player to speak before speaking again.

Variations: Add to the challenge by varying the number of words allowed in each turn. You can limit everyone to one-word sentences or give each player a different number of words to say (no more than five). The most complicated variation involves a sliding scale: On the first turn, players say one word, the next turn is two words, then three, and so on, until players get to five. Then the number of words decreases by one each turn until it goes back to one.

For the Players: Just keep your number of words in mind. It may help to count off the words on your fingers as you speak. Remember not to leave a player hanging. Jump in if a player is out of words, because she can't speak again until someone else does. The faster the dialog the more entertaining it is for the audience—just don't get too far ahead of yourself. Keep the plot going throughout the skit.

small group

Shake Up Your Shakespeare

For the Emcee/Teacher: This game gives players a chance to show they are well-rounded actors by performing Shakespeare. Ask the audience for a setting, making sure you choose a modern one. Now have players perform a scene in that setting, speaking in pseudo-Elizabethan style and throwing in as many Shakespearean stereotypes as they can. For example, a scene set at McDonald's might begin with the line "Forsooth, good traveler, canst I help thee with thine purchase of food that is fast?"

Variation: Choose a famous Shakespeare play and perform a "missing" scene from it. Set the scene in a modern location and away you go. One of our classics is the missing hot tub scene from *Romeo and Juliet*.

For the Players: The game is obvious—just try to talk in a caricature of Shakespearean dialog. Work as many Shakespearean themes into the story as possible: mistaken identity, women disguised as men, witches, and ambition to be king are some good ones. Deliver soliloquies. Throw in some Elizabethan-sounding words and phrases, such as "betwixt" or a well-placed "hey, nonny, nonny." Some players have gotten by in this game by just adding *-eth* to the ends of their verbs ("the sun shineth"). Oddly enough it works. If you really are well-versed in Shakespeare, be careful not to make too many inside jokes. Remember, don't be too serious because this game is done for comedy.

Tips for Teaching: This game is best played at a time when students are studying Shakespeare. Reading a little Shakespeare before jumping into this game is helpful. You'll also find that playing this game makes students more excited to study the real thing.

Bizarre Games

Some would argue that we've already covered some pretty strange games in this book, and they'd be right. But the following games are even stranger. They are some of the truly bizarre games we play in Quick Wits.

I really like the wacky games, because they add another level of fun for the crowd and another level of challenge for the players. And as strange as it might sound, all of these games have been played by children. I guess they have no fear of the bizarre.

Photo by Bob Bedore

Ball of Mucus

For the Emcee/Teacher: This game takes the format of the basic scene game and adds a little touch of *The Twilight Zone* to it. Ask the audience to suggest a room (such as a waiting room, classroom, or shop) as the setting for a scene. In this setting, players should act out a scene that seems ordinary at first. But all is not normal—there is a huge ball of mucus in the middle of the room. All the characters know it's there, but no one wants to admit it. It's the dirty secret they are all trying to hide. During the scene the players will try to avoid the ball, but eventually someone will end up in it. (Perhaps he falls into it, or perhaps he is pushed.) What the other players do is up to them. They can save the person or just leave him there to be a part of the dirty secret.

For the Players: As you act out the scene, you must constantly try to avoid the ball. Look for ways to use the ball in the scene as well, such as throwing trash into it or using it to moisten envelopes. It's fun to have an "outsider" enter the room and be disgusted by the ball. The others will pretend not to know what she's talking about. They might decide the only way to keep their secret is to feed the outsider to the ball and pretend that she was never here. Strange events always seem to happen around the ball of mucus.

groups
of 3

Bucket of Water

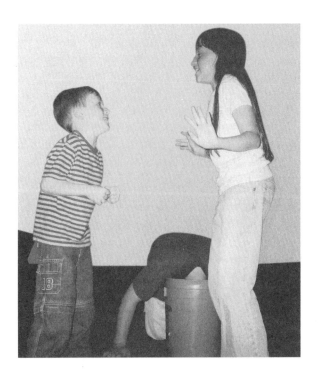

Props: a bucket filled with water (or another substance—see Variation below)

For the Emcee/Teacher: Ah, I can barely remember life before Bucket of Water. In this game, two players begin a scene on a topic chosen by the audience, while a third waits for her entrance "offstage"—but actually, in the middle of the stage with her head stuck in a bucket of water. She waits for one of the other players to tap her and take her place. Then she will have to come up with an excuse as to why she is wet: "Wow, it's really pouring out there," or "I've got a really bad sinus infection," or whatever fits into the spirit of the scene. The game goes on like this, with players taking turns in the bucket, until the scene reaches a satisfactory conclusion.

Variation: We've played this game with all sorts of things in the bucket—everything from Bucket of Snow to Bucket of Milk and Cookies to Bucket of Whipped Cream. You can do just about anything, as long as players always justify why they're covered with snow, whipped cream, or whatever it is, each time they come up from the bucket.

For the Players: Don't drown. It will mess up the comedy. In truth, if you stick the top part of your head in the water you should be able to keep your mouth out of the water, thus creating the illusion that you're holding your breath for a long time. Just don't let the audience know or you're sunk (pun certainly intended). When a player is in the bucket, he is considered offstage, even though he's right in the middle of the stage. This provides perfect exits and entrances. An obvious gimmick is to leave one of the players in the bucket for a while. This player can wave his arms to attract attention and then take a huge breath when he finally comes up.

Tips for Teaching: Younger students will want to play this game right away because they love the idea of getting wet. Make it clear that the object of the game is not to find out who can hold her breath the longest. The game is really about the scene and thinking of ways to explain being wet. Make sure that players remain safe. Players should tap other players out of the bucket quickly, and anyone who is having trouble should come up right away, even if he hasn't been tapped. Remind students that they can "cheat" by putting only the tops of their heads in the water, leaving them free to breathe through their mouths.

Dead People

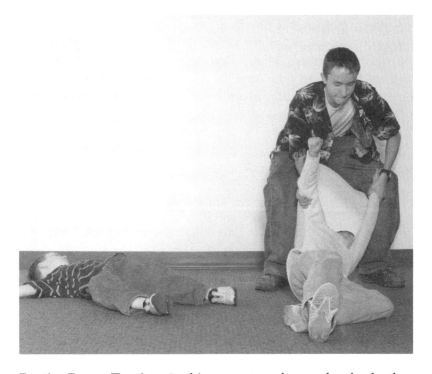

For the Emcee/Teacher: In this game, two players play dead—they are stiff or floppy corpses with no independent power of movement. The third player acts like a puppeteer making the bodies move. He also speaks for them (sometimes moving their lips at the same time). Using this strange method, the three players must act out a scene based on a movie, a historic event, or an everyday situation, as suggested by the audience.

Variation: With younger players, you might decide to play this game in groups of four, so that each "dead body" has its own puppeteer. This variation may help students play more safely. (See **Tips for Teaching** on the next page.)

For the Players: This game is in the hands of the puppeteer—literally. That being the case, the key for the puppeteer is to put the players into fun situations. Try to make both "dead" players stand up at the same time. Have them interact with each other. The more movement you can create, the more the audience will enjoy the  scene. If your scene is based on a movie, don't try to do the entire story. Just go for a scene that works well. Most important, as the puppeteer you need to be careful. Dead People has caused more blood to be spilled than all other games combined. The "dead" players can prevent injury by secretly helping the puppeteer. Let the puppeteer move you; the game is not interesting if it is impossible. If the puppeteer is trying to make you stand up, help by subtly adjusting your position so

 that you will not just fall over right away. You can look dead and help the puppeteer at the same time.

Tips for Teaching: Stress that nobody wants to get hurt. The "dead" players should never let go completely of their self-control—just enough to make it look convincing. Likewise, the puppeteer should never let them fall. After they have worked together for a while, the players will get a feel for Dead People, but stress safety in this game from the beginning.

Evil Twin

For the Emcee/Teacher: Have two players act out a scene based on an ordinary situation chosen by the audience, such as a first date. All is not as it seems, though: One of the players has an evil twin. Every once in a while her twin (the third player) tags her out and takes her place. The evil twin pretends to be the good twin, but makes mischief and causes embarrassing problems. The good twin doesn't want anyone to know about the evil twin, so when she returns she must try to patch things over and make up excuses for "her" evil behavior. For example, the evil twin might come on during the first date and dump the soup all over her date's head. After returning, the good twin might explain this by saying that she recently read a report that clam chowder is good for the skin.

Variation: Add to the fun by playing in groups of four and giving evil twins to both players in the scene.

For the Players: If you are playing the good twin, you can give the evil twin an opportunity to enter by saying that you have to leave for a moment. Then your evil twin can knock you out and take your place. Balance the time onstage between good twin and evil twin. This game is not just about evil—it is about mopping up after evil. As the evil twin, let the scene develop for a while between your entrances.

Tips for Teaching: This is a good game for helping students understand the concept of justification (making everything make sense in the context of the scene). You can help put students in the right frame of mind with this exercise: Give them an example of a bizarre event. Now ask them to make up reasons why this bizarre event might actually be "a good thing."

93

groups
of 4+

Hecklers

For the Emcee/Teacher: This game is really a staged version of the TV show "Mystery Science Theater 3000," in which a space traveler and two robots are forced to watch the worst B-movies ever made. The trio show up as silhouettes at the bottom of the screen, and they heckle the movie, shouting wisecracks.

To play the game, have a group of players leave the stage and join the audience. Ask the audience to choose a topic for a scene, and invite another group of players up to perform the scene. The group onstage does not perform the scene for laughs; they present a serious, even action-packed scene. They should pretend to be bad actors in a bad movie, and the players in the audience should heckle them. If you need a demonstration, just rent an episode of "Mystery Science Theater 3000" (MST3K) on video.

For the Players: The hecklers need to make sure they don't talk over each other. This can be hard, because the same clever idea may come to two hecklers at once, and you'll both want to shout it out. If you have said a lot already, hold back and give the other hecklers a chance. As for the players onstage, your real job is to set up jokes for the other team. Don't talk too fast, and leave some space between your lines so that the hecklers have a chance to get wisecracks in. You can help by giving the hecklers some easy setups: "I have something to tell you," "I can't...I can't...I can't...," and "What am I going to do now?" are examples of lines that can be followed by a good heckle. Also, make exaggerated gestures for the hecklers to mock. A pointed figure can always be followed with "Pull my finger." The more you give the hecklers to work with, the better.

Tips for Teaching: Make sure students are familiar with "Mystery Science Theater 3000" before they play the game. Show them a video if necessary. And make sure they don't talk over each other. If this becomes a problem, go back to Counting on You (Game #6).

small group

Superhero Eulogy

For the Emcee/Teacher: Ask the audience to come up with a name for a superhero (let's say Lactose Intolerant Man). Sadly, this superhero has recently passed away. Players will act out his funeral; each will play a character who crossed paths with the hero. Players could be the hero's sidekick, spouse, or boss—or even the super villain who is glad to see the hero gone.

For the Players: Before beginning the scene, quickly plan your characters together, making sure you have a good variety. That way you won't end up with three sidekicks. When improvising your speech, try to keep it to a minute or less. Puns are the key. Use the name of the hero to make up as many puns and other jokes as you can. "It might sound cheesy, but Lactose Intolerant Man was the cream of the crop. Who'd have thought he'd ever curdle up and die?" The player who speaks last has the hardest job, because by then usually all the good puns have been taken. Make sure the last player has a really good character to play. You might not expect a scene that is nothing more than a funeral for a superhero to get big laughs, but it always does.

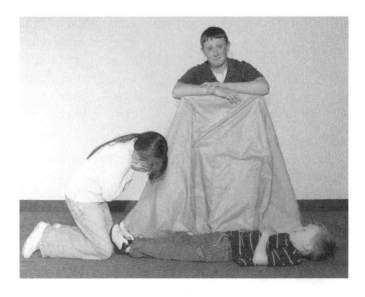

Line-up Games

All of these games place the players side by side in a line onstage. One at a time they step forward to deliver their joke or pun. Unlike most improv games, these don't involve much teamwork. Each game is a series of brief solo performances.

Some younger students may find these games a little intimidating at first because they have to step out alone, but they'll come along. Act as if everything they say is great. This will build their confidence and help them find their way.

Teamwork does come into play in these games in one important way: Sometimes a few seconds go by before anyone can think of a good joke. Rather than leave the audience hanging in silence, an actor can step forward and tell a joke that he knows is dumb, just to buy some time for the other actors. At Quick Wits we call this "taking a bullet." I'm proud to say that I've taken a great many bullets over the years.

Bunch
of Blanks

For the Emcee/Teacher: The typical bar joke begins, "A bunch of
_____s walk into a bar...." That's why this joke-based game is
called Bunch of Blanks. Ask the audience to fill in the blank with an
occupation, animal, or character type. Have players stand in a line
across the stage and come forward one by one whenever they are
inspired. Players will have to come up with jokes about the subject the
audience chose, using the basic bar joke format:

A bunch of Titanic passengers walk into a bar and order drinks,
saying: "Hold the ice."

A bunch of doctors walk into a bar, and the bartender says that
they'll have to wait for a seat. The doctors reply, "It's okay, we have
plenty of patience."

A cowboy walks into a bar-and-grill and sits on the stove. The bartender asks if he'd prefer a stool, and the cowboy answers, "No, I'm
home on the range."

For the Players: Wordplay is the key to this game. Go for the puns
and twist words around. Think your joke through so that you won't
trip over the words as you deliver it. Listen to the other jokes to make
sure you don't repeat any. Don't worry about a joke bombing. If you
sell it, even a terrible joke will still work.

96

Wearing Many Hats

Props: a big box of hats and wigs, most with obvious uses (fire hat, royal crown, etc.)—the more hats the better

For the Emcee/Teacher: Place a big box of hats and wigs onstage and ask the audience for a topic (like bad blind dates, or Presidential candidates). Have the players stand behind the box and rummage through the hats, looking for inspiration. One by one, players should step forward and use the hats to act out anything related to the topic.

For the Players: Most of the hats will have obvious uses. Don't be afraid to go for the obvious, but look for other ideas that can work as well. In a cowboy hat you can obviously be a cowboy, but you could also be George W. Bush. The same wig could make you into a glamorous woman, or a professional wrestler. A baseball cap worn to the front could make you a player, or it could make you a rapper if worn to the side. You could even put two baseball caps together (one facing front, one back) to make a Sherlock Holmes hat. Don't repeat. Be creative!

Hot Spot

For the Emcee/Teacher: Designate a spot at center stage as the "Hot Spot." Choose a player to stand in the Hot Spot and sing about a topic the audience chooses. The player should sing the first song he can think of that has anything to do with the topic. The other players should stand near the Hot Spot and listen to the song. The topic, lyrics, style, or writer of the song should quickly inspire another player to think of a different song. For instance, "Somewhere Over the Rainbow" might lead to "The Rainbow Connection." The first player to think of a new song pushes the singer out of the Hot Spot and starts singing her own song. Players should keep replacing each other and singing new songs until you call an end to the game.

For the Players: Listen for keys words in a song to spark your choice of a new song. If you can't think of anything, think of songs in the same style, or other songs by the same artist. Don't hog the Hot Spot. If you've been singing a lot, hold back for a few songs to give others a chance. If the game has gone on for a while and someone comes up with a great song, it is fun to have everyone join in singing that song. A mass sing-along is a great ending to the game.

Pile
of Props

Props: a wide variety of objects

For the Emcee/Teacher: Throw a pile of props on the stage. Players should look through the props, thinking of unusual ways to use them. Whenever inspiration hits, a player should step forward with her prop, demonstrate the use, and tell what it is. For example, a player might pick up an ordinary book, hold it open over his head, and call it a small roof. Another might pretend to throw the book like a Frisbee and call it an early design for a Frisbee. Another might prop the open book on the floor in front of her and call it a small wall holding back a giant. Another might open and close it like a gobbling mouth and call it a flat Pac-Man. Another might hold it open over his chest and call it a bad bulletproof vest. Another player could call it a police weapon, hitting someone lightly over the head with it and saying, "Book 'em." The possibilities are endless.

Variation: You can create special "nonsense" props for this game—objects with interesting shapes, but without any predetermined use. Players can use the same nonsense object over and over, coming up with myriad uses.

For the Players: Really open your mind and try to see the objects differently. Pay attention so you don't repeat what another player did.

Tips for Teaching: Have kids practice this game a lot. It's a good way to train them to think creatively and change their perspective. In a classroom setting, you might seat students in a circle and have them pass an object around. Each player must use the object for something other than its intended use before she can pass it to the next person. Each player's unusual use for the object doesn't have to be clever, it just has to be different. This game helps teach students that the point of improv is using your imagination, not just being funny.

Scenes Not Seen

For the Emcee/Teacher: Ask the audience for a popular movie or television show. Choose a drama if possible, because it is so hard to satirize a comedy. Players must step forward one by one (or a few at a time) and act out "missing" scenes from the drama, each just one or two lines long. Here are a few examples of possible scenes not seen in *Titanic*:

A concerned crewmember shouts: "There's an iceberg back there…and it's gaining on us!!!"

Two panicked penguins waddle around, saying: "Cruise Ship!! Cruise Ship!!"

Rose: "I'll never let go, Jack." Jack: "Don't you think you could just move over a little bit? I mean, there's room for two on that thing."

A passenger says to his date: "You had to order extra ice with your drink, didn't you?!"

A passenger calmly says: "Hey, an iceberg." Then he sticks his tongue out and mimes licking it. His tongue gets stuck and the iceberg drags him away.

For the Players: Listen to the other players' scenes so that you won't repeat their ideas. When you step forward to do a short scene, don't be afraid to pull another player up to do the scene with you.

This game is all about making fun of scenes and plot elements that the audience will recognize. An obscure joke will almost never work. Try to make sure your scene will be funny to anyone who saw the previews for the movie, not just to fans who watched the whole movie twice. In fact, you can play this game even if you haven't seen the movie yourself. For instance, even if you haven't seen the blockbuster *Titanic*, you probably know that the movie involved a love story set on a boat that hit an iceberg and sank. You may even know famous lines, like "I'm king of the world!" and "I'll never let go, Jack," and famous scenes like the one in which Jack sketches Rose. You can use all that to make up scenes you haven't seen for yourself.

Unlikely Slogans

For the Emcee/Teacher: Ask the audience to suggest a well-known product. Have players stand in a line onstage and think up slogans that have never been—and would never be—used to advertise that product. Whenever inspiration strikes, individual players should step forward to announce their slogans.

For the Players: Think about the product and what it does; then come up with a slogan that would be completely wrong for that product. For example, an eyewash could have the following slogan: "Now in new spicy Cajun." If you're having problems thinking up ideas, use slogans that would be terrible for any product. The slogan "Now with 30 percent less glass" would work for any food product. Listen to the other players' jokes to make sure you don't repeat one. If a product has a familiar slogan in real life, just saying the opposite of that slogan will get a laugh.

World's Worst

For the Emcee/Teacher: In Unlikely Slogans (Game #100), players thought up the world's worst slogans for particular products. This game lets players think up other "world's worsts." You might have the audience suggest an occupation (doctor, for example) or an event (perhaps a wedding). Players will think up examples of the world's worst doctors, or the world's worst things to overhear at a wedding. As in the other Line-up Games, players should stand in a line and step forward as they think up worsts.

An obvious example for world's worst doctor would be: "Well, the operation is complete. Let's put it down as ending at...at.... Say, has anyone seen my watch?"

For the Players: As always, pay attention to what the other players are doing. Never repeat a joke. Puns and stereotypes about the occupation will get you through the game. Don't be afraid to make a dumb joke, because a groan is almost as good as a laugh. Remember—if your joke bombs, sell it even harder. The audience will be with you in the end.

Bonus Game

The following is a game that I developed as a tool for writers, but it has proved fun in the classroom as well. I've included it here as a little bonus to say thank you. Enjoy.

Storython

The World's Easiest No-Paper, No-Game Master Role-Playing Game

The Basics

In Storython, players work together to tell a story. Each player adds a sentence to the ongoing story until everyone agrees that the story has reached its perfect ending.

That's the game in a nutshell—now let's look into it in more depth.

How to Play

To begin with, the players all agree on a setting and a genre for their story. Storython can be played in any genre (even Jane Austen if you are in that frame of mind), so have fun and try them all.

Then players should decide how the story will reach its end. You might decide to place a time limit on the story, or agree on a condition that must be met. For instance, a horror story might end when there is only one character alive, or a mystery story might end when the crime is solved. This is all agreed upon by the group so that we don't have to have a Game Master.

Now pick one person to start. She begins the story by setting the scene and introducing her character, providing as much description as is possible in the one-sentence structure. Going around the circle, each of the other players uses his first sentence to introduce his own character and what his initial take on the scene might be.

To continue, just keep going around the circle, with each player adding one sentence at a time. Every player must include their own character in their sentence.

Challenges

Of course, players will create plot twists that others disagree with. Each player has two chances to challenge another player's sentence. To challenge a sentence, a player has to announce the challenge and then play a quick game of Rock-Paper-Scissors against the other player. If the challenger wins, the challenger substitutes a new sentence for the one he challenged. The new sentence must include the general theme of the other player's sentence, but can make the outcome a bit more favorable for the challenger. If the challenger loses the game of Rock-Paper-Scissors, the sentence stands as is. If Rock-Paper-Scissors ends in a tie, the challenged sentence is ignored, but the challenger also loses his own turn. Use challenges wisely, since you only have two.

Advanced Rules

After the group has agreed on the genre, setting, and ending conditions for the story, players write down (in secret) three goals they want to accomplish by the end of the game. Once the game is over, the players reveal their lists. Whoever met the most goals wins the game. In the case of a tie, the other players vote to choose the winner.

What's a Sentence?

Okay, we all know what a sentence is, but this game might push that a bit. Obviously, many players will use run-on sentences to get the most out of each turn. Just try not to overdo it. Should a "sentence" get too long-winded, the other players can call for a halt. Then the player must decide whether to end the sentence there, or try again and reword it more concisely. But the purpose of the game is to tell a good story, so give a little and just enjoy the ride.

Antics for the Advanced

Now that you understand how to do improv, you really want to make it shine. You want to do magic.

I once heard a magician talking about those "Secrets of Magic Revealed" television shows that tell everyone how a trick is done. He said the shows don't bother him, because magic is like a violin. You can show someone how to play a violin. You can even teach the person to draw the bow across the strings while forming simple chords with the other hand. That person may know how the violin is played, but it takes a real master to make the music come to life. The same can be said for magic—and for improv, too.

To become an improv master, you must remember that an improv scene is a mini-play. Just going up onstage and being silly is not enough. Your little improvised scene should have all the components of a full-scale play—characters; setting; and a plot with conflict and a beginning, a middle, and an end. You just don't get to read the script to find out what happens.

Character

Improv is all about making choices. The most important choice in a scene is the very first one you make: Who are you? A character's identity affects every reaction he makes and every word he says during the scene. So you have to choose that identity before you say your first word.

When you begin doing improv, you will probably perform your first few scenes as a character who is nearly, if not wholly, you. That is the easiest way to make it through the scene. You are familiar with yourself and know instinctively how you would react in a given situation. Playing yourself at first is fine, because it helps you get used to doing improv, but eventually you'll have to break out of being just you. Being someone else, even someone slightly different, will change your reactions to people and events. For example, I don't play many broad, wacky characters onstage. The differences in my characters come from the inside—from different motivations. A new motivation turns a character into a completely different person. Let's say you are afraid of heights. If you are playing a character who is essentially you, and you pretend to be on the ledge of a tall building, you will act scared. But if you decide to play a character who is some sort of thrill seeker, you will play the scene differently. Most people are first attracted to acting by the liberating idea of a world where you can be someone different than who you are. Take advantage of that world.

Sometimes the hardest part of creating characters is coming up with ideas. I simply watch people. My favorite place is a shopping mall. I love to watch how people react to others and to situations. Most of them react differently than I would, so I can file those ideas away and use them onstage. I can pick up dozens of characters in a busy location. It's like guilt-free stealing.

When you are playing character types, such as pirates or fashion models, don't be afraid of stereotypes. Some teachers balk at the idea of using stereotypes, but I look at it from an audience perspective: The audience expects certain types to act in certain ways. I'm sure very few pirates walked with peg legs and said, "Arrgh, me mateys!" but the audience can identify with that character quickly and accept it. On the other hand, playing the exact opposite of a stereotype can also work well. An erudite pirate who can't understand his shipmates' quaint jargon and ponders why they are wearing peg legs in a time of huge advancements in the field of prosthetics can work well. The key is that the audience knows the stereotype, so they can recognize its opposite.

Once you have chosen your character's identity, you need to know the character's attitude. This is made up of two points—emotion and motivation. Without an attitude, there is no character. Why is the character the way she is? How does she feel about the situation she finds herself in? How does she feel about the others on the stage? These are not only important questions, but also they make up the entire foundation of the character. If you know the answer to those questions, you can react to whatever is thrown your way. On this foundation you can build any scene necessary.

Voice and Body

The voice is your best tool for creating a character. A few words out of your mouth should give the audience, and the other actors onstage, a sense of who you are. Again, I invite you to listen to people. Hear how they talk and the way their voices change in different situations. Emotions affect the voice a great deal. Angry people speak in loud voices, excited people talk quickly, sad people talk slowly, and so forth. But your character's identity also affects his voice. Think about people who are leaders. Their voices have the ring of authority. They speak confidently and purposefully. Whether they really know what they are talking about is unimportant; they believe they do, and will talk forever on the subject—and most people will listen.

Pay attention to speech patterns as well, because little things like favorite phrases can help define a character. Listen to a child tell a story. Count how many times the child says, "And you know what?" in the middle of the story. Adults would not usually use that expression, but children use it to show their wonder. In your choice of words and phrasings, be sure to play to the mental level of the character. If you are playing a child, don't use sophisticated vocabulary. Use phrases that people might expect to hear from someone of your character's age, sophistication, and education level. Use speech patterns to flesh out a character without having to create a whole backstory. And don't forget about the pitch of your voice. Changes in pitch can help define the character type. A weightlifter with a high squeaky voice is very different from one with a low bass. A librarian who can't control his loud voice gives you an interesting foundation for a character. As I said, little things can make a big difference.

Accents can also help define a character. But take my advice: Make sure you feel confident with the accent before you rush out onstage to use it. Learning an accent is easy for some, and a nightmare for others. Accents become easier if you use our improv friend, the stereotype. Sure, all southerners may not really say "y'all," but this is something that the audience will expect. In fact, one of Quick Wits' most popular games—Silly Accents (Game #59)—involves changing accents every fifteen seconds or so. We tell the audience that our nickname for this game is "Offend Everyone." The game isn't truly offensive, but the accents we use will stereotype everyone. Knowing a little about the region where an accent originates can also help you sell it to the audience. Many of my actors have trouble doing an authentic Canadian accent, but they know they can talk about hockey, back bacon, and the like, and survive for a short time. Whatever you do, don't forget the first rule of accents: Know the accent well before you do it onstage. You'll be glad you followed the rule.

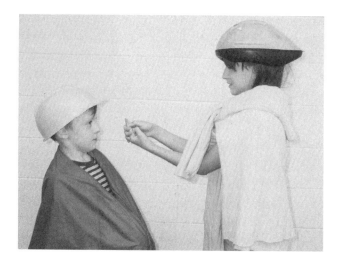

Along with your voice, use your body to help portray your character. All of the same exercises you did to develop your character's voice—people-watching, thinking about emotions and identity, and so on—will translate perfectly to the way you use your body. Take a Walk (Game #1) is designed to help you get a feel for using your body to portray emotion and character. In a scene, your character will do much more than walk: be ready to make all sorts of motions in character. Even the way you sit in a chair will tell us a lot about your character. The most important factors that will affect your character's body are emotion, motivation, gender, and age. A confident person holds himself differently than someone who is sneaky. The same can be said of an older person and a child. All the little things come together to create the whole.

Last but not least—just do it. Show the audience who you are, don't tell them. The audience doesn't want a play-by-play of what you are doing. Don't say that you are an old person. Just be one.

Stay True to Your Character

Once you have made your choices about your character, stick with them. Nothing looks worse onstage than an actor dropping out of character or playing against her own character. This brings the scene to a halt, and it takes a while to get things going again.

An improv audience is so accepting. Be anyone onstage and the audience will stay with you, as long as you believe it and are faithful to the character.

A character may work so well that you want to reuse it in other skits. Some people feel that bringing characters back is not true improv, but I disagree. I believe that as long as you place the character in a different situation, you are most certainly doing improv. In fact, I love to see a character brought back. It's like seeing an old friend again and watching her new adventures.

One Moment of Character Magic

Whenever I think about character work and how little things can mean so much, I'm always drawn to one scene. It is one of the most magical character moments I've ever seen onstage. We were playing "Random Game Show," a bizarre game in which the audience makes up the name of a game show and we play it. The name of the game show that night was "Whose Underwear Is It Anyway?" and I was playing the game show host. We were in the "Name the Celebrity" round, when I hold up imaginary underwear and the contestants buzz in to answer. One of the actors, Cameron Stewart, was playing an old man named Harold Winthrop III. Harold has fought in just about every war and has had several of his body parts replaced, or just removed. This character is the perfect study of body and voice. I held up what would be the biggest panties in the world (I know, not clever) and was just hoping for a cheap laugh. But then Cameron/Harold went berserk. He started ranting: "Where did you get those panties? It isn't right!" He claimed that they were his late wife Mildred's underwear, and said I had no right showing them in public. He went on to say that she was a lovely, fine woman, who didn't deserve this humiliation. The most amazing part was that Cameron was doing a funny "old man rage" bit, but there was such love and sadness behind it as well.

Reading this account, you might not understand that the audience was doubled over with laughter—the character is that good— but I can tell you what I saw. I was actually caught up in Harold. Here was a man who had such love for this woman, and every bit of it came through. Cameron never dropped the character. Even in the anger there was the confusion of the moment. He didn't leave what he'd been doing in the early part of the game to pursue this new element, he merely added it. Cameron added one little bit of information, and suddenly I knew so much about Harold. Harold Winthrop III is still a funny character to watch, but now every time Cameron plays him I can't help but think about Mildred and what the two of them shared.

It was a perfect improv moment.

The Straight Man

There is one character who never gets talked about—the straight man, or non-character. This character is a vital component to a scene. In a sense he is the embodiment of the audience. He is the everyman who has strange things happen around him or *to* him on occasion.

I'm lucky to work with wonderful actors who are constantly looking for new character types to play, so I often take the noncharacter role. It's one I like. It allows me to keep a scene on track and set up the characters for the big laughs. Just keep in mind that to make a scene with wild characters truly funny, there has to be one person onstage to act as the foil. Don't forget the straight man.

Be Your Character from the Start— Unless You Have to Be Someone Else

You should have your character well established in your mind before you enter. The moment you hit the stage, be that character completely. If your character needs to have a special relationship to the other characters onstage, be sure to let the actors know in some way. You don't have to say "I'm your mother"—you should always try to show who you are instead of telling it straight out, unless that's the only way people will understand. Instead, take a subtler route. You can establish that you are the characters' mother by saying something like "Your father and I . . . ." Showing an exaggerated emotion can also help you define your character for the others onstage.

Have your character in mind, but be prepared for a shock. Other actors may give you a character before you have a chance to do anything. I've seen it happen far too often. For instance, you might enter a scene all set to be the jealous boyfriend, but the first thing you hear when you walk onstage is: "Dad, what are you doing here?" This simple line just changed your character from the boyfriend to the dad. You need a new character right away! Don't panic, just think quickly about what your motivation might be. Are you happy with your daughter or angry with her? Become the new character immediately. Still, you don't have to throw the idea of the boyfriend out the window. As the dad you can point out to the daughter that she has a jealous boyfriend, and the conflict can still take shape.

The point of what I'm saying is twofold. First, establish who you are quickly so that the other actors can accept you. Second, if the others establish a character for you, you have to be that character. Never say, "I'm not your dad, I'm your boyfriend!" You are whoever the other actors say you are.

Environment

Any class I teach has the word *environment* pounded into them. The ability to conjure up an environment separates the beginners from the seasoned improvisers. It is another key to creating magic. In most improv shows the stage is blank, but it doesn't have to remain that way. That bare stage can be anywhere, and anything can exist on it. All you have to do is make it so.

Remember, all improv scenes should include characters, plot, and setting (environment). Character and plot are easy. Even if you don't have much of a character, the moment you open your mouth and speak your character begins to form. As the characters interact, a plot is also set in motion. But unless you make a point of constructing an environment brick by brick, the characters and plot will exist in a vacuum. Thankfully, the audience is very accepting. If you tell the audience that there are palm trees growing in the middle of your living room and then look up at the swaying fronds, the audience will see them. A world can be built with just a look and a few words—sometimes even with just the look.

Here is an exercise you can easily try with a class or troupe. Have one or two actors do a scene set in a given public location. Their goal is to establish as much environment as possible in one minute. They don't have to create a plot, just the environment. As they act out the scene, count how many environmental aspects they establish. You'll be sur-

Photo by Charlie Ellis

prised how low the number is. The actors think that they are doing a lot, but until they really concentrate, the number is usually lower than ten. Now have them try the exercise again, using the same location. The number of environmental elements should be higher. Then hold a contest: challenge all the actors to try the exercise, and see who can come up with the most environmental elements in their location. You can give actors hints to help them develop a richer environment. For example, actors might earn one point for saying that a store sells candy. But actors could add quite a bit more by acting as if the candy counter goes on for miles and exclaiming as they point out the different brands they can see. Actors can start building environment the moment they enter a scene. They could just open a door, or they could add a little more to the scene by making the sound of jingling bells as the door opens.

When I demonstrate this exercise for my students, I challenge them to think of a location where I can't produce much environment. So far they haven't come up with anything to stump me. It's not that I'm brilliant, I just know the best rule of environments: Anything Is Possible. I can have anything with me onstage. Once students tried to stump me with the location "floating in space." Of course I pointed out all the things I saw and reacted to them, but then I turned to my space suit. I played with a few gadgets here and there on my suit, and then I discovered a special pocket—one I hadn't seen before. I opened the pocket, and there was a self-inflating space ship. I pulled the cord and watched it expand. It was huge. I got in and inspected the ship. It had all kinds of decks with elevators and stairs to use; a transporter for traveling to various locations; a live theater with a show in progress; a huge dining hall; and even an exercise room, complete with a pool. All of that materialized in a minute.

Environment is where improv can be the most magical. Wonderful worlds can suddenly appear in front of the audience, all with the power of suggestion. And it is these little journeys to new worlds are what people expect when they come to the theater.

Use the Entire Stage

Many actors get caught up in their dialog and forget about stage movement. Maybe it's the director in me, but I insist that my actors move around the stage. Sure, in real life we might stand in the same position to talk to someone for a few minutes, but it makes the scene boring for the audience.

One easy way to keep moving is to use the environment you create. Even doing something simple like turning on the tap to get a glass of water can create movement and add a little touch of realism to a scene. Establish the environment early, so that you can use the stage throughout the scene. Just make sure you don't establish a sink onstage left, and later wash your hands onstage right. The audience will remember where the object is—if you're wrong it takes them out of the scene. Try to remember where everything is.

Here's a fun little exercise to get people used to moving around onstage. Tell them to work as a group to form a letter (such as *H* or *L*). Without talking, they should arrange themselves into the shape of that letter. Once the letter is complete, tell players to remember the spot where they are standing. Next, give the group a few more letters to form. They should remember their spots for each letter. Have them run through the letters a few times so that their positions are firm in their minds. Now have some fun. You might assign a certain emotion to each letter and have the actors walk to their spots showing that emotion. Or you might change the way the actors feel about each other. It's great to form a letter while everyone is terrified of each other. You can also split the class and have half form one letter (showing one emotion) while the other half has a different letter and emotion. This exercise is not only useful for improv; it also helps actors build blocking skills for plays and the like.

You Don't Have to Be a Mime

While acting in the environment around you, don't think that you have to be some sort of expert mime to make it work. The simple act of pretending to push a button, for example, is something anyone can do. The same can be said of loading clothes in a washer, bathing a dog, or walking on the moon. All it takes is a belief from you to make it so.

I remember a scene that involved a boss talking to an employee. The boss wanted to make a point, so he drew back the curtains and asked the employee to look out the window. The employee looked way down, as if they were on the top floor of a huge building. The boss took it further by opening the window and making a simple move to step out onto the ledge. The employee followed, and they did a portion of the scene with a confident boss easily traipsing on the ledge while the employee clung for his life. It wasn't great mime, but it was a wonderful scene. The suggestion was all that was necessary to make the whole thing believable.

The Scene

Once you create characters and environments, it's time to make something happen. This is where scene work comes into play. Every scene should tell a story. Although short, the story should have a plot, just like a regular play. This means that it needs a conflict and a beginning, a middle, and an end. The story must move in a natural progression so that the audience can follow it.

In the Beginning...

The beginning of a scene is all about establishing character and environment quickly. Since you've been working on these, the beginning should be easy for you. As with character, the first choices you make about a scene are the most important. Once you have established characters and environment, the audience will be looking to you for some clue as to what is about to happen. You have to make important choices: Do you start the scene onstage or off? Is the catalyst—the event that sets the plot in motion—about to happen, or has it occurred just before the scene opens? Reacting to what is going on can be easy; sometimes the hardest part of improv is getting it going in the first place.

The audience wants to know about your character, and you should have some sort of backstory in mind. Still, it's not wise to go into your history. The obvious reason is that you don't have the time to do this, but, in addition, backstory just isn't that important to most scenes. If there is some history that makes you the way you are and you feel it is needed in the scene, look for the places in the scene to bring it out. These little glimpses of your past are far more compelling than a complete disclosure.

Keeping the Scene Going

The best way to keep the scene moving forward is to remember the rule of "Never Say No." In case you have forgotten (or thought you were too good and didn't read Building Blocks for Beginners), this rule is one of acceptance. There is no denying what another actor has brought to the scene. If an actor does deny something, the scene comes to a screeching halt—and everyone is left trying to figure out a way to get it started again. Always work with what you are given and adapt constantly. This acceptance will keep the scene moving forward, and quite possibly take all of you places you wouldn't even have thought about. Speaking of thought, don't think too far ahead in a scene. The scene should unfold in front of you and the audience. Trying to plan often leads to disaster, because your expectations will rarely be met. Plan out your beginning in a scene and then ride the scene out.

An entrance by a new character can also help keep a scene moving forward. We usually perform three-actor scenes in Quick Wits, and often the third actor will hang back and look for an opportunity to come into the scene. Of course, the actor needs to come in with a purpose—and the timing should be perfect. Entering a scene is like surfing. The wave is coming, and it's your job to pick the right time and join it. A surfer knows that if she is too soon or too late dropping in, she won't be riding that wave. To enter a scene, you really have to pay attention to what is happening onstage. Make sure that the actors onstage are in a position to accept a new character, and that your character will fit in with what is happening. Also make sure that you establish your character and your role in the scene quickly, unless you have some reason to be mysterious. Sometimes the actors onstage signal a new actor to come in. Be ready to use lines like "Here she comes now" or "Sssh, the police are coming" as your cue to come in—and with a ready-made character.

Exiting a scene can be just as important as entering, and the same rules about timing have to be followed. Exits should be strong and have purpose; the other actors should know that you've left and why.

Entrances and exits are also a great way to establish more environment. They give you more locations where you could go if necessary. If a character comes in from a snowstorm, everyone could decide to go out into the snow.

Conflict in a Scene

When a skit lasts only a few minutes, something needs to happen right away. Conflict is one of the best ways to get it going. Now, this doesn't mean I think that there should be a fight in every scene, because conflicts can be subtle.

Take a scene about cheerleaders for example. The conflict could be personal, such as a rivalry between two people competing for the last spot in the cheering squad. The conflict could spur cooperation, if it pits all the characters against an unseen opponent. The whole squad could be working on a routine to beat another team in a future competition. The conflict could even be generated by something bizarre, such as an alien trying to fit in as a cheerleader. Actually, the scene could be about two rival cheerleaders at a competition who have to work together to create a cheer that would repel the alien invasion.

Just don't get caught up in the idea that conflict has to be violent or negative. Every second of the day we face some sort of conflict. In fact, we can't take a step when we walk without first falling forward and hoping that our foot will be there to catch us. Without conflict, there is no plot. And without the plot, there is nothing to resolve at the end.

Whatever You Are Doing…Sell It!

Regardless of what you are doing, you have to do it with conviction and sell it with everything you have. This is true for scene work in improv just as much as one-liners. If you have a character, be it. If you have a joke, tell it. To quote the famous Jedi master, "There is no try."

An audience member once pointed out that one of my actors would tell a joke, get a small reaction from the audience, and look hurt before sulking toward the back; while another actor would get the same reaction and accept it as if it were a standing ovation. That's the key. The really good improvisers know that they can't hit the target every time, so they keep firing just as hard with each line and look for the big score. The attitude has to be, "Oh yeah? Well, you've laughed at me before and you'll laugh at me again."

It's especially important to sell your line when you're taking a bullet for the team. As I explained in the Line-up Games, this is a phrase we use when an actor says something—anything—just to buy some time for the others. The actor knows the line won't be funny, but he has to sell it to the audience as if it's hilarious. This comedic sacrifice ensures that the audience has something to watch at all times. To return to the magic trick analogy, this is a classic case of misdirection.

Photo by Bob Bedore

Let the audience watch someone bomb like a pro instead of watching a group of actors standing there trying to think up something.

The End

Being able to end a scene well is the mark of a great improviser. Some improv games have a built-in ending, but most do not. A scene should always end when it reaches its natural resolution, or its highest point. Your job is to get it to one of those.

Reaching the end can be tough. Here you are creating dialog from thin air; now you must not only follow whatever strange scene has developed, but bring it to its conclusion. It's like getting in a plane you've never seen before and being told to bring it in for a landing. The best advice I can give you is to look for opportunities to present themselves. If an interesting conflict is in motion, all you have to do is resolve it. If the scene has no conflict, create one and resolve that. If your leader or emcee is on top of the scene, you can end it with a good line that will get a big laugh. With any luck the emcee will take the opportunity to stop the scene.

Scenes: Love Them or Leave Them

If a scene is not going well, you can change it. That may sound strange, but you've already learned that anything can happen onstage, and that you can create any environment—use this to your advantage. When you find yourself in a scene that's going nowhere, you might discover a secret vortex in the pantry that can take you to any place or time. Or

you might simply open a letter announcing that you are the winner of a fabulous trip departing immediately. These new settings give you a fresh start with characters that you've already established. Speaking of characters, you can change them as well. I've often seen actors pretend to rip off a mask (or pull a zipper on a full body costume) to reveal a different character. It's a great escape that gives the scene a little jolt.

Remember that when a scene goes badly you can take one of two options: you can go down with the ship, or you can see it as a challenge for a fresh start. After my first few times going down with the ship I vowed never to let it happen again.

Creating Magic

Now you have all the essential elements of an improv scene: character, environment, and plot. Here are more tricks of the trade that will help you dazzle audiences with your sleight of hand.

Mental Lists

One of my personal tricks to doing improv is making lists in my head. I'm sure many performers do this naturally. I simply use that little bit of time before a scene begins to create a mental list of ideas that go with the suggestion. I'm not talking about making specific plans, just mentally gathering material. It's like putting my brain on notice that I might need some information on this subject quickly. Let's say the scene is about plumbing. I go through a list of the types of tools that a plumber might carry. I also think about objects that might be found in a bathroom, or things that might cause a plumbing problem. Finally, I give a quick thought to ways to escape the scene if it goes wrong.

You don't have a long time to think before a scene begins, often just a few seconds, but you can train yourself to make lists quickly. Try it right now. Give yourself an occupation and think of everything associated with that occupation. Now try it with an activity or a location. The more you practice, the faster you can generate these lists.

Singing Games

I find mental lists to be especially helpful in Singing Games. These can be the hardest of all games to play onstage. That's because so many elements go into creating a song. With most singing games, you have to tell a little story, think up rhymes, and try to stay on some sort of pleasant pitch—all at once. Doing this well is the Holy Grail of improv.

The key to a singing game is the rhyming scheme. Here is my trick: Once I know the subject of the song, I put together my mental list. Then I can pick out a few words from the list that are easy to rhyme. I keep those words in mind throughout the song. This way, if I get stuck I can end a sentence with one of the words and know that I'll be able to rhyme it in the next sentence.

My other secret is to work on each phrase backwards. Starting with the last word in a phrase lets you work toward something definite. Take the plumber example: In looking over the list of words my mind created, I pick "commode." It's a funny word and has rhyming possibilities. I know I'm going to end with the word, so now I have to figure out how to get there. First I decide on the rhyming word—"explode." From there the phrase comes quickly: "I can look at you and see you're about to explode/So let me in right now, and I'll fix your commode." It's not going to win a Grammy, but it will get you going.

When you sing a song, pay attention to your accompaniment. I usually listen for a few seconds before singing, so I can get a feel for the song. There is no need to rush into the song—take that time to make it as good as you can.

Plan Ahead

After the emcee takes a suggestion from the audience, a few seconds always pass before the scene begins. Use them wisely. Make your character choices, plan an entrance, make mental lists.

Once you have an idea, quickly tell another actor about it before the scene starts. You don't have to plan out an entire improv together. If you have an idea about entering as the mother, just whisper to the other actors, "I'm coming in as the mom." Now they can be ready for you. Communication is especially important for beginners. Improv is hard enough without having two people on different pages at the start of the scene. If you share information, you are well on your way toward creating a scene.

Props and Costumes

Props and costumes are instant scene builders. At Quick Wits we keep boxes of strange items for the actors to twist with their imaginations. We have few realistic props, for the simple reason that if you bring a realistic prop into a scene it negates all of the "fake" ones onstage. Let's say you're doing a scene about robbing a bank. One actor has a realistic gun, and the other is using a hose as her gun. Now you have to spend time explaining the hose. If both actors have hoses and pretend they're guns, they're guns, and that's that.

Even a simple thing like bringing a real suitcase onstage and filling it with imaginary clothes is a stretch. It's better just to mime both the suitcase and the clothes and move on. But "fake" props can be so great. We have some long flotation devices that look like tubes—I'm not even sure if they have a real name—and they have been used for more things than I could count. Each time they are used, the audience buys into them.

Costumes are great for improv. We are always looking through the thrift stores for the next great item. Throwing on a flowery dress is a perfect way to become the mother. You can change yourself from improv actor to host of a snobby review show in an instant, just by slipping on a tweed jacket. I also suggest having simple bits of fabric for the actors to use. These can be turned into just about anything in an improviser's hands.

Bending the Rules

Now it's time to take another look at the basic rules of improv and tweak them a little. Improv rules were made to be bent, if not broken.

The first rule to bend is the "Never Say No" rule. Yes, I think it's important—but it's not the be-all, end-all improv rule. If improv is supposed to be a slice of life, then we must do the things that we do in life. And sometimes we say no. Here's an example of taking this rule to the extreme: I was watching a class. The instructor had pounded the "Never Say No" rule into the students, and would stop a scene whenever they said no. Two actors were playing a scene about taking drugs. Another actor came in and was told that it was his turn to do drugs. The actor froze for a moment, and then reluctantly did as he was told. After the class, I asked him about the scene. He told me that he had planned to come in as one character's brother and convince him not to do drugs, but he was afraid to say no. The scene didn't go well, and he felt like he had ruined it. All the actor had to do was tell the other actor, "No! I won't take the drugs, and you shouldn't either…because I love you, brother," and an interesting conflict would have taken shape. But he couldn't, because he wasn't allowed to say no.

Remember, you are your own character, with your own set of emotions. If someone says you have a duck on your head, you can't deny it (unless you point out that it's actually a duck decoy, and you're hoping to attract ducks to your head). But if someone says you *like* to have ducks on your head, you can examine your character and decide for yourself whether that is the case. There is a big difference.

The other rule I like to bend from time to time is "Don't Ask Questions." If you look at some other resources on improv (and I hope you will), you'll see that everyone hates questions. The usual reason people give is that asking questions forces actors to come up with an answer. But that's the whole point of improv: You're constantly coming up with ideas off the top of your head. If you can't come up with an answer, it's because you don't have a grasp of your character. I tend to look at a question as an invitation. If someone asks me something, I have the ability to assess the situation and give a response based on what is happening. Sure, it's no fun always having to answer questions, but just think of what might happen if you come onstage and the first thing you hear is, "Why are you covered in cheese?" An entire scene can develop from your answer.

The last bendable rule is "No Clipping." Truth be told, you should only bend this rule with actors you know well. If I know the abilities of the actors I'm onstage with, I have no problem clipping them within those abilities. It's fun, it keeps all the actors on their toes, and it heightens everyone's awareness. But even then you have to be careful, because a clip can always come back at you. Imagine that you're interviewing someone and you've just brought up the fact that she used to dance. You ask her to show everyone a little taste of her dancing; then she reminds you that she only danced ballroom style, and she needs a partner. Now you have to dance with her. If you decide to clip others, expect that they may clip you back. When you break the "No Clipping" rule, you have to consider the Golden Rule. Do unto others as you would have them do unto you.

Having Fun

An improviser is just a person on a stage with no set, no props, and no script. You have to do whatever it takes to survive. And that survival instinct is what will keep you alive through the scene.

Don't try to remember every rule. It's too hard. After a while it will all come naturally to you. But until then, this is the most important rule to remember: Don't worry about the rules—have fun.

Putting On a Show

Back when I started Quick Wits, there was no improv in my area. Soon people saw what we were doing and tried to start their own troupes. Unfortunately, we made it look too easy, and they didn't see all the subtle things that go into a night of improv. I don't want you to make the same mistake.

Much like a magic act, improv is only easy after you know what you're doing and have practiced it down to an art form. But even if a magician does the most amazing tricks in the world, she will not sell tickets if she can't reach her audience properly.

Forming a Troupe

You may be a teacher with no intention of forming an improv troupe, but this section is still important reading. The class is a troupe, and you should treat it as one.

When people are forming an improv troupe, often the first mistake they make is that they just look for funny people and stick them together. When I first started doing improv I was a stand-up comedian. My promoter came up with the idea of putting all of his comedians onstage together to do some improv. It never really worked. Sure we were all funny, but each comedian was trying to get his own one-liner out there for a laugh. We were never a team.

The troupe has to be a team, and each member has to have a specific role. You can't have a team of all the same types onstage, just as you can't have a sports team of all goalies. You need people who are the wild types, people who do wacky characters, and people who do physical comedy. My style is that of a straight man. I like to keep the scene together, and I take great pride in setting up other actors for jokes or situations. I always love to have someone who can play a musical instrument onstage as well. The point is to have a well-rounded cast, so that you can do different types of comedy and make it all work.

It's important for the troupe to get along. In a play you can hate your leading lady, but you can still get by because your character loves her. This doesn't work in improv. When people who want to join Quick Wits ask me what they have to do, I usually tell them to hang out with us for a while. The Quick Wits troupe is made up of friends, and we get together all the time. Unfortunately for those around us, we are always "onstage." There are several local places where everyone shudders when we come in.

Your troupe has to have a good (if not great) offstage relationship for many reasons. The first is trust. If you are going to go on a blank stage and try to create a funny scene with people, you have to trust that they're going to be there for you. Friends in a troupe also develop a sixth sense about each other, the way twins do. After a troupe has been together for a while, you start to know what everyone is thinking. You can anticipate what is about to happen. Just the other night an audience member swore that we had rehearsed our entire show. We took that as a compliment, but we're just a group of actors who know each other very well. The last reason to be friends is sometimes the hardest to take. During a show your fellow actors may say much that is unflattering to you. As I near forty, my six-pack stomach looks more like a keg, and it has become the target for abuse. We make fun of each other's body types, hair colors, dating habits, and whatever else is handy. Our whole aim is to make the audience laugh, and everything about us is fair game. Because we are friends, we don't take offense.

Here's one more element to keep in mind as you form a troupe: The troupe should have a solid leader. This doesn't mean that the leader is the only voice of the troupe, but rather that there is one person who always keeps an eye on the big picture and works for the best interests of the troupe.

Practice

Once you form a troupe, make sure you get together as much as possible at first. You will be working on games and improving your performance, but you will also be doing something even better—learning about each other. A troupe has to know what to expect from one another. It's useful to know your fellow actors' interests, strengths, and weaknesses. Maybe an actor in your troupe is a history nut. If you

set him up with events from history, you can be sure that he'll know what you're talking about and run with it. All sorts of hobbies, talents, and interests can provide material for the show. Conversely, if you know your fellow actors' weaknesses, you can avoid topics they know nothing about.

Be sure to structure your rehearsal so that all the actors feel their time is well used. I recommend making time for actors to bring up games or things they want to work on. Don't just say, "We'll work on it next week." Work on it right away, while it's fresh in their minds, and they'll be more apt to learn. Keep the practices light and allow for input from the whole group. That way they grow as a team and don't just look to one person for guidance. There will come a time when the leader is not there. When that happens, you don't want the other actors to be looking around blankly, waiting for instructions that are never coming.

While I do feel that practice is necessary, I also believe that there comes a time when your troupe should get together less and less. Otherwise they will lose some of the spontaneity they once had. When you've reached this point, it is best to use practices as a chance to try out new games or maybe work on a few areas where the group seems to be getting lax. You want to keep improv fun, so get together as a group and do just that: have fun. In a non-performance environment you'll see that the actors will still act out characters and try to make each other laugh, but it isn't a rehearsal. By getting together socially, you can sneak in some practice without getting burned out on improv.

The Emcee

Here is another area where many troupes trip up. The emcee is the most important part of the show, and the most often overlooked. The emcee, of course, is the master of ceremonies. While the actors are focusing on one scene, the emcee is juggling a longer list of duties. These include monitoring the audience to see what is working and what is not, explaining the games, taking suggestions from the audience, keeping an eye on the actors to make sure they are holding up and maintaining the rules of improv, dealing with "rowdy" audience members, keeping up the pace of the show, monitoring the show's length, deciding when skits should end, and sometimes even dealing with little things like spills in the theater that need to be cleaned up. It's no wonder I have a hard time convincing actors to emcee shows.

So how do you emcee an improv show? It's a tough question, because I feel emcees are 90 percent born and only about 10 percent made. You've got to have a special ability to work a crowd. You always have to keep in mind that you are the one who gets the audience from point A to point B, but they aren't likely to remember you were there. In fact, if the audience remembers the emcee better than they remember the actors, you've done a bad job. I have been an emcee as well as an improviser, so I'll pass on my advice.

The emcee's first job is taking suggestions for settings, situations, and so on from the audience. These suggestions give actors the gas to fuel their skit. In many troupes, emcees have a policy of taking the first suggestion called out. This strategy has its drawbacks—the first being the obvious, that the idea may really stink for the game you are playing. The actors have to trust that the emcee is going to give them something good to work with. The other drawback is that the audience will notice that you always take the first suggestion, and will be less likely to yell out additional suggestions. If a great idea comes to someone, it's too late. Give the audience a moment to think about the question posed to them. Still, you have to take something before too much time goes by. Think about the game that is being played; as soon as you hear a suggestion that will work for that game, take it. The directions for the specific games in this book include some advice on choosing suggestions. Also keep in mind that the actors like to be challenged—try to choose a suggestion that is very different from the suggestion used the last time actors played a particular game.

The emcee's hardest job is ending the skits. Some skits have a built-in ending, but others last until the emcee stops them. It's your call whether to wait for the scene to resolve, or end it at its climax. When I emcee, I watch a scene from the beginning and look for the buildup. When I see a big laugh, I'll make a quick judgment as to whether or not I think something else is coming. If not, I'll end the scene right there. In improv, always try to follow the old rule of leaving an audience wanting more. It's a tough call, but one that gets easier to make as time goes on. On several occasions I've had actors tell me that I ended a scene too soon, and that they were working on something. I remind them: the scene ended on a big laugh, they couldn't guarantee another one like that, and they can always file away what they were going to do for another time. That's another great thing about improv—you'll always get a second chance.

Scenes that aren't going well are even tougher to end. It's hard to watch a scene that's not funny, just looking for some moment, any moment, to kill it. You want the actors to get some type of reaction from the crowd before halting the scene, but you worry that if you wait too long you're only prolonging the suffering—for the actors and the audience. In cases like this, just hope that the actors will reach into their bag of tricks for an easy laugh, and you can end the skit there.

Dealing with hecklers in the audience can also be hard on the emcee. If you ignore them, they usually get much louder before they go away, but if you respond directly to what they said, they've won. The best solution is to try to get rid of them with a simple one-liner in response. It lets the audience know that you heard what the heckler

said and that it won't work. Saying something like "I'm not sure if that was a suggestion or just a cry for help" will usually do the trick. If you ask for a hobby or occupation and hear a loud off-color remark, you can say, "It doesn't have to be *your* occupation; it can be anything." This works well because it gets a good laugh and everyone is happy. Another tactic is to speak about the people (or date) the heckler is with. Commenting on how proud they must be will usually get them to shut the person up for you. If all else fails, just let the heckler know that you'll never take a suggestion like that and it would save him a lot of time to stop yelling it—short of that, you can have him removed. It's harsh, but I've had to do it. We don't have too much trouble at Quick Wits, because the audience knows that we try to run a clean show. In fact, in a few pages you'll see what we do when people, including audience members, cross the line.

Keep in mind that being an emcee requires practice. Make sure that you know the games really well and can explain them to the audience in the shortest time possible. I've built up a mental script for each game and just rattle it off almost word for word each time. When I emcee a show, all I want to do is keep the show rolling along without getting in the actors' way. All I ask from the actors is that they don't upstage the game introductions. It's a good relationship and it works.

The Show

Every improv show is different, so deciding what your show will be like is up to you. When Quick Wits was formed, I looked at all the sources I could find and went from there. Then I changed the show to try to get a little more energy out of the troupe. I even had to put together a whole new cast at one point, so I tweaked the show to take advantage of the strengths of the actors I now have. I would invite you to do the same thing. Go to see as many improv shows as you can, and watch how each troupe has put its show together. What do they do about lighting and sound? How do they handle suggestions? Are the actors onstage or off when not performing? There are lots of choices to make.

I chose a competitive format for our Quick Wits show. This means that we have two teams of actors compete against each other to see who can make the audience laugh most. The competition looks real enough, but it always comes down to the final round to see who wins it all. There is a fair amount of banter between the teams, but real fans know the banter is as much a part of the show as the games we play. I like this format because of the energy it gives. We may not be able to play quite as many games as we could if we just rattled them off one right after another, but the upside for us is far greater. The format lets the actors be themselves in front of the audience between games, and that creates an important connection between actors and audience.

To maintain this connection, we keep the actors onstage at all times. When actors aren't doing a scene, they sit off to the side and watch the other team play. It's great to see the off-duty actors fall on the floor laughing when something hilarious has just happened onstage, or simply applaud with the audience after a fun skit. It also shows the audience that we're all in this together and keeps the actors "real" to them.

We use lighting and sound to keep up the pace of the show. Some troupes will end a scene with a blackout, but we don't. I love that moment when the scene is over and the actors drop the characters they were playing to laugh, do a high-five, or whatever. It's a magical part of the show and I want the audience to see it, so we keep the lights up full throughout the show. Sound is important, too. We play loud recorded music after a scene to keep the energy going between games. Often the actors break into improvised dance numbers with the music. It's a little extra treat for the audience. Our sound guy does a great job—I'm amazed at the songs he finds to tie into the scene that just played—but I'd love to have a full-time keyboardist playing along with the scenes. I just haven't found the right person yet. Use a keyboardist if you can; this adds an extra layer to the scenes and opens up more possibilities.

Quick Wits is set up for audiences of all ages, and we have boundaries about adult subjects and language. That doesn't mean that we are squeaky clean, we just see who is in the audience and play to them. We even set up a rule: if an actor oversteps any line and says something that the audience doesn't like, the audience is free to yell for a "Penalty." When this happens, the audience will tell the actor what he has to do to earn their forgiveness. We've had some pretty tough penalties, so the actors stay out of trouble for the most part. We made the same rule apply to the audience, so if an audience member steps out of line we can call for a penalty on her.

I've had people tell me that there should be no bounds on improv, and that the actors should say what they want. Some say that I'm blocking actors' creativity by placing restrictions on what they can say. But I look at it this way—a lion in a cage will explore every inch of that cage, but a lion that is free will usually stick to his favorite ground. I feel actors have to be more creative when faced with parameters. Besides, I like having my kids sit in the audience of my shows. The "freedom of content" was one of the reasons why I got out of stand-up comedy.

Quick Wits is the "fast food" of comedy improv. We hit the stage and take hold of the audience quickly. We don't let go until we leave. Of course, you don't have to do your show the same way we do. That's the beauty of it all: You can do anything. Find what works for you, your troupe, and your audience. Then go out there and make it happen.

Just remember that no matter what you do, it's genius. It's brilliant! It's improv.

Photo by Charlie Ellis

SmartFun activity books encourage imagination, social interaction, and self-expression in children. Games are organized by the skills they develop and simple icons indicate appropriate age levels, times of play, and group size. Most games are noncompetitive and require no special training. The series is widely used in schools, homes, and summer camps.

101 MUSIC GAMES FOR CHILDREN: Fun and Learning with Rhythm and Song by Jerry Storms

All you need to play these games are music CDs and simple instruments, many of which kids can make from common household items. Many games are good for large group settings, such as birthday parties, others are easily adapted to classroom needs. No musical knowledge is required.

>> 160 pages ... 30 illus. ... Paperback $14.95 ... Spiral bound $19.95

101 DANCE GAMES FOR CHILDREN: Fun and Creativity with Movement by Paul Rooyackers

These games encourage children to interact and express how they feel in creative ways, without words. They include meeting and greeting games, cooperation games, story dances, party dances, "musical puzzles," dances with props, and more. No dance training or athletic skills are required.

>> 160 pages ... 36 illus. ... Paperback $14.95 ... Spiral bound $19.95

101 DRAMA GAMES FOR CHILDREN: Fun and Learning with Acting and Make-Believe by Paul Rooyackers

Drama games are a fun, dynamic form of play that help children explore their imagination and creativity. These noncompetitive games include introduction games, sensory games, pantomime games, story games, sound games, games with masks, games with costumes, and more. The "play-ful" ideas help to develop self-esteem, improvisation, communication, and trust.

>> 160 pages ... 30 illus. ... Paperback $14.95 ... Spiral bound $19.95

101 LANGUAGE GAMES FOR CHILDREN: Fun and Learning with Words, Stories and Poems by Paul Rooyackers

Language is perhaps the most important human skill, and a sense of fun can make language more creative and memorable. This book contains over one hundred games that have been tested in classrooms around the world. They range from letter games to word play, story-writing, and poetry games including Hidden Word and Haiku Arguments.

>> 144 pages ... 27 illus. ... Paperback $14.95 ... Spiral bound $19.95

For more information visit www.hunterhouse.com

YOGA GAMES FOR CHILDREN: Fun and Fitness with Postures, Movements and Breath

by Danielle Bersma and Marjoke Visscher

An introduction to yoga for children ages 6–12, these games help young people develop body awareness, physical strength, and flexibility. The 54 activities are variations on traditional yoga exercises, adjusted for children and clearly illustrated. Ideal for warm-ups and relaxing time-outs.

>> 160 pages ... 57 illus. ... Paperback $14.95 ... Spiral bound $19.95

101 IMPROV GAMES FOR CHILDREN AND ADULTS *by* Bob Bedore

Improv comedy has become very popular, and this book offers the next step in drama and play: a guide to creating something out of nothing, reaching people using talents you didn't know you possessed. Contains exercises for teaching improv to children, advanced improv techniques, and tips for thinking on your feet—all from an acknowledged master of improv.

>> 192 pages ... 65 b/w photos ... Paperback $14.95 ... Spiral bound $19.95

101 LIFE SKILLS GAMES FOR CHILDREN: Learning, Growing, Getting Along (Ages 6–12) *by* Bernie Badegruber

How do you teach tolerance and responsibility or help children deal with fear, mistrust, or aggression? Play a Life Skills game with them! You can help children learn social and emotional skills; for example, how to integrate the new girl into the group and safe ways of letting off steam.

>> 192 pages ... 40 illus. ... Paperback $14.95 ... Spiral bound $19.95

101 FAMILY VACATION GAMES: Having Fun while Traveling, Camping or Celebrating at Home *by* Shando Varda

This wonderful collection of games from around the world helps parents to connect with their children. Full of games to play at the beach, on camping trips, in the car, and in loads of other places, including Word Tennis, Treasure Hunt, and Storytelling Starters.

>> 160 pages ... 7 b/w photos ... 43 illus. ... Paperback $14.95 ... Spiral bound $19.95

101 COOL POOL GAMES FOR CHILDREN: Fun and Fitness for Swimmers of All Levels *by* Kim Rodomista

It's never too early to begin enjoying the benefits of water exercise and play. These games for children ages 4 and up can be played again and again. Best of all, they burn calories and improve a child's overall fitness level. A special section covers exercises, including water walking, jumping, and balance activities.

>> 128 pages ... 39 illus. ... Paperback $14.95 ... Spiral bound $19.95

3 1901 04486 0619